RANDOM HOUSE

TREASURY of FAVORITE LOVE POEMS

Random House Treasury of Favorite Love Poems, 2nd Edition

Copyright © 2000, 2004 by Random House, Inc.

This book is available for special discounts for bulk purchases for sales promotions or premiums. Special editions, including personalized covers, excerpts of existing books, and corporate imprints, can be created in large quantities for special needs. For more information, write to Special Markets/ Premium Sales, 1745 Broadway, MD 6-2, New York, NY, 10019 or e-mail *specialmarkets@randomhouse.com*.

Please address inquiries about electronic licensing of reference products, for use on a network or in software or on CD-ROM, to the Subsidiary Rights Department, Random House Reference, fax 212-572-6003.

Visit the Random House Reference Web site: www.randomwords.com

Printed in China

Library of Congress cataloging in publication data is available.

ISBN: 0-375-42602-7

2nd Edition

0 9 8 7 6 5 4 3 2 1

RANDOM HOUSE

TREASURY *of* FAVORITE LOVE POEMS

2ND edition

REVISED BY NATALIA SUCRE

RANDOM HOUSE
REFERENCE

New York   Toronto   London   Sydney   Auckland

CONTENTS

iv

REVISER'S PREFACE

If love is joy, it is also sorrow; if sweet, also bitter; if sublime, also profane. These extraordinary contradictions, like love itself, are the stuff of cliché. Happily, they are also the stuff of poetry—that transformer and transgressor of the commonplace. In these pages, the reader will experience how poets throughout the ages, from various languages and cultures, and from multiple points of view, explore the power of love.

In *Random House Treasury of Favorite Love Poems*, 2nd edition, the poems are divided into sixteen categories that are meant to guide the reader through the range of emotions and situations that love presents. While each category corresponds to a distinct experience of love and, often, to particular poetic conventions in various traditions, the poems themselves often resist such classification. The categories may help guide the reader to certain themes, but inevitably they will commingle in the reading.

While the poems speak for themselves, each category requires a brief explanation:

Joy and Celebration—These are poems of praise and rejoicing not only for a lover, but for love in its own right.

Eros and Longing—These poems represent unnamable, unquenchable desire, constantly attempting to name itself, constantly attempting to end its thirst.

Wooing—Poems of invitation, these implore a beloved to share love and life in open fellowship of varying kinds and under varying circumstances.

Seduction—Here are poems that illustrate the two faces of seduction: well-crafted arguments for lovemaking and (apparently) defenseless surrender to the power of love.

Worship and Devotion—Here are poems of praise dedicated to a lover. Curiously, these acts of adoration are often inspired by rivalry for the heart of a chosen one.

DISCORD—Bickering, squabbling, the immensity of minor differences, and, of course, the all too familiar toxin of jealousy—all are intensified by love as the poems here artfully observe.

COMMUNION—As the religious connotations of this term suggest, love can be an experience of divinity or at least a transcendence of the self. Here, poets explore love as spiritual fellowship.

TORMENT—These are poems of paradox, defying logic in their combination of extreme joy and pain. Here, love is, in a time-honored tradition, madness and folly; above all, it is unfathomable.

ABSENCE AND SEPARATION—Here are poems on the absence of a beloved—whether it be due to circumstance or choice, temporary or permanent.

HOPE—In these poems, love takes on the force of inspiration and expectation, whether it be for the hour of an appointed reunion or an event that will transform one's life completely.

BITTERNESS—These poems explore the resentment of a lover scorned or the anguish of a love disappointed.

DISAVOWAL—Here, poetry expresses how love can be at its strongest just as one is making a definitive break with it.

SORROW AND LAMENTATION—These poems are of absence, separation, loss—common sources of sorrow in love.

TENDERNESS—These poems are in the line of lullabies. Here is a love that requires care, attention, love, song.

TRANSIENCE—In these poems, mortality serves as a backdrop to love that is both enduring and fleeting.

REMEMBRANCE—Love lost and love ended distinguish these elegiac poems.

NATALIA SUCRE
Decorah, Iowa

JOY AND CELEBRATION

Invitation to Love

Come when the nights are bright with stars
Or come when the moon is mellow;
Come when the sun his golden bars
Drops on the hay-field yellow.
Come in the twilight soft and gray,
Come in the night or come in the day,
Come, O love, whene'er you may,
And you are welcome, welcome.

You are sweet, O Love, dear Love,
You are soft as the nesting dove.
Come to my heart and bring it to rest
As the bird flies home to its welcome nest.

Come when my heart is full of grief
Or when my heart is merry;
Come with the falling of the leaf
Or with the redd'ning cherry.
Come when the year's first blossom blows,
Come when the summer gleams and glows,
Come with the winter's drifting snows,
And you are welcome, welcome.

—*Paul Laurence Dunbar*

The Canonization

For God's sake hold your tongue, and let me love,
    Or chide my palsy, or my gout,
My five grey hairs, or ruined fortune flout,
    With wealth your state, your mind with arts
        improve,
        Take you a course, get you a place,
        Observe his Honour, or his Grace,
Or the King's real, or his stamped face
    Contemplate; what you will, approve,
    So you will let me love.

Alas, alas, who's injured by my love?
    What merchant's ships have my sighs drowned?
Who says my tears have overflowed his ground?
    When did my colds a forward spring remove?
        When did the heats which my veins fill
        Add one more to the plaguy bill?
Soldiers find wars, and lawyers find out still
    Litigious men, which quarrels move,
    Though she and I do love.

Call us what you will, we are made such by love;
    Call her one, me another fly,
We are tapers too, and at our own cost die,
    And we in us find the eagle and the dove,
        The phoenix riddle hath more wit
        By us; we two being one, are it.
So to one neutral thing both sexes fit
    We die and rise the same, and prove
    Mysterious by this love.

We can die by it, if not live by love,
    And if unfit for tombs and hearse
Our legend be, it will be fit for verse;
    And if no piece of chronicle we prove,
        We'll build in sonnets pretty rooms;
        As well a well wrought urn becomes
The greatest ashes, as half-acre tombs,
    And by these hymns, all shall approve
    Us canonized for love:

And thus invoke us; 'You whom reverend love
   Made one another's hermitage;
You, to whom love was peace, that now is rage;
   Who did the whole world's soul contract, and
      drove
      Into the glasses of your eyes
      (So made such mirrors, and such spies,
That they did all to you epitomize,)
   Countries, towns, courts: beg from above
   A pattern of your love!'

—*John Donne*

Us

I was wrapped in black
fur and white fur and
you undid me and then
you placed me in gold light
and then you crowned me,
while snow fell outside
the door in diagonal darts.
While a ten-inch snow
came down like stars
in small calcium fragments,
we were in our own bodies
(that room that will bury us)
and you were in my body
(that room that will outlive us)
and at first I rubbed your
feet dry with a towel
because I was your slave
and then you called me princess.
Princess!

Oh then
I stood up in my gold skin
and I beat down the psalms
and I beat down the clothes
and you undid the bridle
and you undid the reins
and I undid the buttons,
the bones, the confusions,
the New England postcards,
the January ten o'clock night,
and we rose up like wheat,
acre after acre of gold,
and we harvested,
we harvested.

—*Anne Sexton*

Out of Catullus

Come and let us live my Deare,
Let us love and never feare,
What the sowrest Fathers say:
Brightest *Sol* that dies to day
Lives againe as blith to morrow,
But if we darke sons of sorrow
Set; o then, how long a Night
Shuts the Eyes of our short light!
Then let amorous kisses dwell
On our lips, begin and tell
A Thousand, and a Hundred, score
An Hundred, and a Thousand more,
Till another Thousand smother
That, and that wipe of another.
Thus at last when we have numbred
Many a Thousand, many a Hundred;
Wee'l confound the reckoning quite,
And lose our selves in wild delight:
While our joyes so multiply,
As shall mocke the envious eye.

—*Richard Crashaw*

Love

Love bade me welcome; yet my soul drew back,
   Guilty of dust and sin.
But quick-eyed Love, observing me grow slack
   From my first entrance in,
Drew nearer to me, sweetly questioning
   If I lacked anything.

"A guest," I answered, "worthy to be here";
   Love said, "You shall be he."
"I, the unkind, ungrateful? Ah, my dear,
   I cannot look on Thee."
Love took my hand, and smiling did reply,
   "Who made the eyes but I?"

"Truth, Lord, but I have marred them; let my
shame
   Go where it doth deserve."

"And know you not," says Love, "who bore the
    blame?"
    "My dear, then I will serve."
"You must sit down," says Love, "and taste My
meat."
    So I did sit and eat.

—*George Herbert*

from *The Song of Solomon*

My beloved spake, and said unto me, Rise up, my
    love, my fair one, and come away.
For lo, the winter is past, the rain is over and gone;
The flowers appear on the earth; the time of the
    singing of birds is come, and the voice of the
    turtle is heard in our land:
The fig tree putteth forth her green figs, and the
    vines with the tender grape give a good smell.
    Arise, my love, my fair one, and come away.
O my dove, that art in the clefts of the rock, in
    the secret places of the stairs, let me see thy
    countenance, let me hear thy voice; for sweet
    is thy voice, and thy countenance is comely.
Take us the foxes, the little foxes, that spoil the
    vines; for our vines have tender grapes.
My beloved is mine, and I am his: he feedeth
    among the lilies.

Until the day break, and the shadows flee away,
turn, my beloved, and be thou like a roe or a
young hart upon the mountains of Bether.

—*from* THE AUTHORIZED VERSION

The Sun Rising

Busy old fool, unruly sun,
　　Why dost thou thus,
Through windows, and through curtains
　　call on us?
Must to thy motions lovers' seasons run?
　　Saucy pedantic wretch, go chide
　　Late school-boys, and sour prentices,
　Go tell court-huntsmen, that the King will ride,
　Call country ants to harvest offices;
Love, all alike, no season knows, nor clime,
Nor hours, days, months, which are the rags of
　　time.
　　Thy beams, so reverend, and strong
　　Why shouldst thou think?
I could eclipse and cloud them with a wink,
But that I would not lose her sight so long:

If her eyes have not blinded thine,
  Look, and tomorrow late, tell me,
Whether both th'Indias of spice and mine
  Be where thou left'st them, or lie here with me.
Ask for those kings whom thou saws't yesterday,
And thou shalt hear, All here in one bed lay.

  She'is all states, and all princes, I,
    Nothing else is.
Princes do but play us; compared to this,
All honour's mimic; all wealth alchemy.
    Thou sun art half as happy as we,
      In that the world's contracted thus;
    Thine age asks ease, and since thy duties be
    To warm the world, that's done in warming us.
Shine here to us, and thou art everywhere;
This bed thy centre is, these walls, thy sphere.

—*John Donne*

Love Lives

Love lives beyond
The tomb, the earth, which fades like dew.
I love the fond,
The faithful, and the true

Love lives in sleep,
The happiness of healthy dreams
Eve's dews may weep,
But love delightful seems.

'Tis heard in Spring
When light and sunbeams, warm and kind,
On angels' wing
Bring love and music to the mind.

And where is voice,
So young, so beautiful and sweet
As nature's choice,
Where Spring and lovers meet?

Love lives beyond
The tomb, the earth, the flowers, and dew.
I love the fond,
The faithful, young and true.

—*John Clare*

Jenny Kiss'd Me

Jenny kiss'd me when we met,
    Jumping from the chair she sat in;
Time, you thief, who love to get
    Sweets into your list, put that in!
Say I'm weary, say I'm sad,
    Say that health and wealth have miss'd me,
Say I'm growing old, but add,
        Jenny kiss'd me.

—*Leigh Hunt*

A Birthday

My heart is like a singing bird
  Whose nest is in a water'd shoot;
My heart is like an apple-tree
  Whose boughs are bent with thickset fruit;
My heart is like a rainbow shell
  That paddles in a halcyon sea;
My heart is gladder than all these
  Because my love is come to me.

Raise me a dais of silk and down;
  Hang it with vair and purple dyes;
Carve it in doves and pomegranates;
  And peacocks with a hundred eyes;
Work it in gold and silver grapes,
  In leaves and silver fleurs-de-lys;
Because the birthday of my life
  Is come, my love is come to me.

—*Christina Rossetti*

Corinne's Last Love Song

I

How beautiful, how beautiful you streamed upon my sight,
  In glory and in grandeur, as a gorgeous sunset-light!
  How softly, soul-subduing, fell your words upon mine ear,
  Like low aerial music when some angel hovers near!
  What tremulous, faint ecstasy to clasp your hand in mine,
  Till the darkness fell upon me of a glory too divine!
  The air around grew languid with our intermingled breath,
  And in your beauty's shadow I sank motionless as death.
  I saw you not, I heard not, for a mist was on my brain—
  I only felt that life could give no joy like that again.

II

And this was Love, I knew it not, but blindly floated on,

And now I'm on the ocean waste, dark, desolate, alone;

The waves are raging round me—I'm reckless where they guide;

No hope is left to right me, no strength to stem the tide.

As a leaf along the torrent, a cloud across the sky,

As dust upon the whirlwind, so my life is drifting by.

The dream that drank the meteor's light—the form from Heav'n has flown—

The vision and the glory, they are passing— they are gone.

Oh! love is frantic agony, and life one throb of pain;

Yet I would bear its darkest woes to dream that dream again.

—*Jane Francesca, Lady Wilde*

What Can I Do Muslims? I Do Not Know Myself

What can I do, Muslims? I do not know myself.
I am neither Christian nor Jew, neither Magian
    nor Muslim,
I am not from east or west, not from land or sea,
not from the shafts of nature nor from the
    spheres of the firmament,
not of the earth, not of water, not of air, not of fire.
I am not from the highest heaven, not from this
    world,
not from existence, not from being.
I am not from India, not from China, not from
    Bulgar, not from Saqsin,
not from the realm of the two Iraqs, not from
    the land of Khurasan.
I am not from the world, not from the beyond,
not from heaven and not from hell.
I am not from Adam, not from Eve, not from
    paradise and not from Ridwan.

My place is placeless, my trace is traceless,
no body, no soul, I am from the soul of souls.
I have chased out duality, lived the two worlds
    as one.
One I seek, one I know, one I see, one I call.
He is the first, he is the last, he is the outer,
    he is the inner.
Beyond "He" and "He is" I know no other.
I am drunk from the cup of love, the two
    worlds have escaped me.
I have no concern but carouse and rapture.
If one day in my life I spend a moment without you
from that hour and that time I would repent my life.
If one day I am given a moment in solitude with you
I will trample the two worlds underfoot and
    dance forever.
O Sun of Tabriz, I am so tipsy here in this world,
I have no tale to tell but tipsiness and rapture.

—*Jalaluddin Rumi (Translated by Bernard Lewis)*

The Wine of Love

The wine of Love is music,
   And the feast of Love is song:
And when Love sits down to the banquet,
   Love sits long:

Sits long and ariseth drunken,
   But not with the feast and the wine;
He reeleth with his own heart,
   That great rich Vine.

—*James Thomson*

"It lies not in our power to love or hate"

It lies not in our power to love or hate,
For will in us is overruled by fate.
When two are stripped, long ere the course begin,
We wish that one should love, the other win;
And one especially do we affect
Of two gold ingots, like in each respect:
The reason no man knows; let it suffice
What we behold is censured by our eyes.
Where both deliberate, the love is slight:
Who ever loved, that loved not at first sight?

—*Christopher Marlowe*

Love's Calendar

The Summer comes and the Summer goes;
Wild-flowers are fringing the dusty lanes,
The swallows go darting through fragrant rains,
Then, all of a sudden—it snows.

Dear Heart, our lives so happily flow,
So lightly we heed the flying hours,
We only know Winter is gone—by the flowers,
We only know Winter is come—by the snow.

—*Thomas Bailey Aldrich*

"This heart is not"

This heart is not
a summer field,
and yet . . .
how dense love's foliage
has grown.

—*Izumi Shikibu*

Debt

What do I owe to you
   Who loved me deep and long?
You never gave my spirit wings
   Or gave my heart a song.

But oh, to him I loved
   Who loved me not at all,
I owe the open gate
   That led thru heaven's wall.

—*Sara Teasdale*

Sometimes with One I Love

Sometimes with one I love I fill myself with rage
 for fear I effuse unreturn'd love,
But now I think there is no unreturn'd love, the
 pay is certain one way or another
(I loved a certain person ardently and my love was
 not return'd,
Yet out of that I have written these songs).

—*Walt Whitman*

Love Is Enough: Song I

Love is enough: though the World be a-waning,
And the woods have no voice but the voice of
     complaining,
    Though the sky be too dark for dim eyes to
  discover
The gold-cups and daisies fair blooming
  thereunder,
Though the hills be held shadows, and the sea a
    dark wonder,
    And this day draw a veil over all deeds pass'd over,
Yet their hands shall not tremble, their feet
    shall not falter:
    The void shall not weary, the fear shall not alter
  These lips and these eyes of the loved and the
lover.

—*William Morris*

EROS AND LONGING

"Eros has shaken my mind"

Eros has shaken my mind,
wind sweeping down the mountains on oaks

—*Sappho (Translated by Stanley Lombardo)*

The Dream

All trembling in my arms Aminta lay,
Defending of the bliss I strove to take;
Raising my rapture by her kind delay,
Her force so charming was and weak.
The soft resistance did betray the grant,
While I pressed on the heaven of my desires;
Her rising breasts with nimbler motions pant;
Her dying eyes assume new fires.
Now to the height of languishment she grows,
And still her looks new charms put on;
Now the last mystery of Love she knows,
We sigh, and kiss: I waked, and all was done.

'Twas but a dream, yet by my heart I knew,
Which still was panting, part of it was true:
Oh how I strove the rest to have believed;
Ashamed and angry to be undeceived!

—*Aphra Behn*

Cherry-Ripe

There is a garden in her face
  Where roses and white lilies blow;
A heavenly paradise is that place,
  Wherein all pleasant fruits do flow:
    There cherries grow which none may buy
    Till "Cherry-ripe" themselves do cry.

Those cherries fairly do enclose
  Of orient pearls a double row,
Which when her lovely laughter shows,
  They look like rose-buds filled with snow;
    Yet them nor peer nor prince can buy
    Till "Cherry-ripe" themselves do cry.

Her eyes like angels watch them still;
  Her brows like bended bows do stand,
Threatening with piercing frowns to kill
  All that attempt with eye or hand
    Those sacred cherries to come nigh,
    Till "Cherry-ripe" themselves do cry.

—*Thomas Campion*

Elegy 5

In summer's heat and mid-time of the day
To rest my limbs upon a bed I lay,
One window shut, the other open stood,
Which gave such light, as twinkles in a wood,
Like twilight glimpse at setting of the sun,
Or night being past, and yet not day begun.
Such light to shamefast maidens must be shown,
Where they must sport, and seem to be
   unknown.
Then came Corinna in a long loose gown,
Her white neck hid the tresses hanging down:
Resembling fair Semiramis going to bed
Or Layis of a thousand wooers sped.
I snatched her gown, being thin, the harm was
   small,
Yet strived she to be covered there withal.
And striving thus as one that would be cast,
Betrayed herself, and yielded at the last.

Stark naked as she stood before mine eye,
Not one wen in her body could I spy.
What arms and shoulders did I touch and see,
How apt her breasts were to be pressed by me.
How smooth a belly under her waist saw I?
How large a leg, and what a lusty thigh?
To leave the rest, all liked me passing well,
I clinged her naked body, down she fell,
Judge you the rest, being tired she bade me kiss,
Jove send me more such afternoons as this.

—*Ovid (Translated by Christopher Marlowe)*

Song to Amarantha, That She Would Dishevel Her Hair

Amarantha sweet and fair
Ah braid no more that shining hair!
As my curious hand or eye
Hovering round thee let it fly.

Let it fly as unconfin'd
As its calm ravisher, the wind,
Who hath left his darling th'East,
To wanton o'er that spicy nest.

Ev'ry tress must be confest
But neatly tangled at the best;
Like a clue of golden thread,
Most excellently ravelled.

Do not then wind up that light
In ribands, and o'er-cloud in night;
Like the sun in's early ray,
But shake your head and scatter day.

See 'tis broke! Within this grove
The bower, and the walks of love,
    Weary lie we down and rest,
And fan each other's panting breast.

    Here we'll strip and cool our fire
In cream below, in milk-baths higher:
    And when all wells are drawn dry,
I'll drink a tear out of thine eye,

    Which our very joys shall leave
That sorrows thus we can deceive;
    Or our very sorrows weep,
That joys so ripe, so little keep.

—*Richard Lovelace*

The Indian Serenade

I arise from dreams of thee
In the first sweet sleep of night,
When the winds are breathing low,
And the stars are shining bright
I arise from dreams of thee,
And a spirit in my feet
Hath led me—who knows how?
To thy chamber window, Sweet!

The wandering airs they faint
On the dark, the silent stream—
The champak odors fail
Like sweet thoughts in a dream;
The nightingale's complaint,
It dies upon her heart;
As I must on thine,
Oh, beloved as thou art!

O lift me from the grass!
I die!   I faint!   I fail!

Let thy love in kisses rain
On my lips and eyelids pale.
My cheek is cold and white, alas!
My heart beats loud and fast;—
Oh! press it to thine own again,
Where it will break at last.

—*Percy Bysshe Shelley*

"Wild Nights—Wild Nights!"

Wild Nights—Wild Nights!
Were I with thee
Wild Nights should be
Our luxury!

Futile—the Winds—
To a Heart in port—
Done with the Compass—
Done with the Chart!

Rowing in Eden—
Ah, the Sea!
Might I but moor—Tonight—
In Thee!

—*Emily Dickinson*

from *Rubaiyat*

A Book of Verses underneath the Bough,
A Jug of Wine, a Loaf of Bread—and Thou
  Beside me singing in the Wilderness—
Oh, Wilderness were Paradise enow!

—Omar Khayyám

"I cry your mercy"

I cry your mercy—pity—love!—aye, love!
   Merciful love that tantalizes not,
One-thoughted, never-wandering, guileless love,
   Unmasked, and being seen—without a blot!
O! let me have thee whole,—all—all—be mine!
   That shape, that fairness, that sweet minor zest
Of love, your kiss,—those hands, those eyes divine,
   That warm, white, lucent, million-pleasured
 breast,
Yourself—your soul—in pity give me all,
   Withhold no atom's atom or I die
Or living on perhaps, your wretched thrall,
   Forget, in the mist of idle misery,
Life's purposes,—the palate of my mind
   Losing its gust, and my ambition blind!

—*John Keats*

In the Orchard

Leave go my hands, let me catch breath and see;
Let the dew-fall drench either side of me;
   Clear apple-leaves are soft upon that moon;
Seen sidelong like a blossom in the tree;
   And God, ah God, that day should be so soon.

The grass is thick and cool, it lets us lie.
Kissed upon either cheek and either eye,
   I turn to thee as some green afternoon
Turns toward sunset, and is loth to die;
   Ah God, ah God, that day should be so soon.

Lie closer, lean your face upon my side,
Feel where the dew fell that has hardly dried,
   Hear how the blood beats that went nigh to
swoon;
The pleasure lives there when the sense has died,
   Ah God, ah God, that day should be so soon.

O my fair lord, I charge you leave me this:
It is not sweeter than a foolish kiss?
   Nay take it then, my flower, my first in June,
My rose, so like a tender mouth it is:
   Ah God, ah God, that day should be so soon.

Love, till dawn sunder night from day with fire
Dividing my delight and my desire,
   The crescent life and love the plenilune,
Love me though dusk begin and dark retire;
   Ah God, ah God, that day should be so soon.

Ah, my heart fails, my blood draws back; I know,
When life runs over, life is near to go;
   And with the slain of love love's ways are
 strewn,
And with their blood, if love will have it so;
   Ah God, ah God, that day should be so soon.

Ah, do thy will now; slay me if thou wilt;
There is no building now the walls are built,
   No quarrying now the corner-stone is hewn,
No drinking now the vine's whole blood is spilt;
   Ah God, ah God, that day should be so soon.

Nay, slay me now; nay, for I will be slain;
Pluck thy red pleasure from the teeth of pain,
   Break down thy vine ere yet grape-gatherers
 prune,
Slay me ere day can slay desire again;
   Ah God, ah God, that day should be so soon.

Yea, with thy sweet lips, with thy sweet sword; yea
Take life and all, for I will die, I say;
   Love, I gave love, is life a better boon?
For sweet night's sake I will not live till day;
   Ah God, ah God, that day should be so soon.

Nay, I will sleep then only; nay, but go.
Ah sweet, too sweet to me, my sweet, I know
   Love, sleep, and death go to the sweet tune;
Hold my hair fast, and kiss me through it soon.
   Ah God, ah God, that day should be so soon.

—*Algernon Charles Swinburne*

The Look

Strephon kissed me in the spring,
    Robin in the fall,
But Colin only looked at me
    And never kissed at all.

Strephon's kiss was lost in jest,
    Robin's lost in play,
But the kiss in Colin's eyes
    Haunts me night and day.

—*Sara Teasdale*

Desire

Where true Love burns Desire is Love's pure
   flame;
It is the reflex of our earthly frame,
That takes its meaning from the nobler part,
And but translates the language of the heart.

—*Samuel Taylor Coleridge*

A White Rose

The red rose whispers of passion,
   And the white rose breathes of love;
Oh, the red rose is a falcon,
   And the white rose is a dove.

But I send you a cream-white rosebud,
   With a flush on its petal tips;
For the love that is purest and sweetest
   Has a kiss of desire on the lips.

—*John Boyle O'Reilly*

On a Girdle

That which her slender waist confin'd,
Shall now my joyful temples bind;
No monarch but would give his crown,
His arms might do what this has done.

It was my heavens' extremest sphere,
The pale which held that lovely deer,
My joy, my grief, my hope, my love,
Did all within this circle move.

A narrow compass, and yet there
Dwelt all that good, and all that's fair;
Give me but what this ribbon bound,
Take all the rest the sun goes 'round.

—*Edmund Waller*

Upon Julia's Clothes

Whenas in silks my Julia goes,
Then, then, methinks, how sweetly flows
That liquefaction of her clothes.

Next, when I cast mine eyes and see
That brave vibration each way free,
O how that glittering taketh me!

—*Robert Herrick*

"Sweet, mother, I the web"

Sweet, mother, I the web
　Can weave no more;
Keen yearning for my love
　Subdues me sore,
And tender Aphrodite
　Thrills my heart's Love.

—*M. J. Walhouse*

Sex Question

Is it a question?

_____

I better be getting home.
Okay.
They continued to sit. They were parked way
  out on the highway.
Cold night smell
coming in the windows. New moon floating
  white as a rib at the edge of the sky.
I guess I'm someone who will never be satisfied,
said Herakles. Geryon felt all the nerves in him
  move to the surface of his body.
What do you mean satisfied?
Just—satisfied. I don't know. From far down the
  freeway came a sound
of fishhooks scraping the bottom of the world.
You know. Satisfied. Geryon was thinking hard.
  Fires twisted through him.

He picked his way carefully
toward the sex question. Why is it a question?
   He understood
that people need
acts of attention from one another, does it really
   matter which acts?
He was fourteen.
Sex is a way of getting to know someone,
Herakles had said. He was sixteen. Hot
   unsorted parts of the question
were licking up from every crack in Geryon,
he beat at them as a nervous laugh escaped him.
   Herakles looked.
Suddenly quiet.
It's okay, said Herakles. His voice washed
Geryon open.
Tell me, said Geryon and he intended to ask
   him, Do people who like sex

have a question about it too?
but the words came out wrong—*Is it true
    you think about sex every day?*
Herakles' body stiffened.
That isn't a question it's an accusation. Something
    black and heavy dropped
between them like the smell of velvet.
Herakles switched on the ignition and they
    jumped forward onto the back of the night.
Not touching
but joined in astonishment as two cuts lie
    parallel in the same flesh.

—*Anne Carson*

WOOING

The Invitation
to the Voyage

How sweet, my own,
Could we live alone
Over beyond the sea!
To love and to die
Indolently
In the land that's akin to thee!

Where the suns which rise
In the watery skies
Weave soft spells over my sight,
As thy false eyes do
When they flicker through
Their tears with a dim, strange light.

There all is beauty and symmetry,
Pleasure and calm and luxury.

Years that have gone
Have polished and shone
The things that would fill our room;
The flowers most rare
Which scent the air
In the richly-ceiling'd gloom,
And the mirrors profound,
And the walls around
With Orient splendour hung,
To the soul would speak
Of things she doth seek
In her gentle native tongue.

There is all beauty and symmetry,
Pleasure and calm and luxury.

The canals are deep
  Where the strange ships sleep
Far from the land of their birth;
  To quench the fire
  Of thy least desire
They have come from the ends of the earth.

  The sunsets drown
  Peaceful town
And meadow, and stagnant stream
  In bistre and gold,
  And the world enfold
In a warm and luminous dream.

There all is beauty and symmetry,
Pleasure and calm and luxury.

—*Charles Baudelaire*
(Translated by J. C. Squire)

A Ring Presented to Julia

Julia, I bring
   To thee this ring,
Made for thy finger fit;
   To show by this
   That our love is
(Or should be) like to it.

Close though it be,
   The joint is free;
So when Love's yoke is on,
   It must not gall,
   Or fret at all
With hard oppression.

But it must play
   Still either way,
And be, too, such a yoke
   As not too wide
   To overslide,
Or be so strait to choke.

So we who bear
This beam must rear
Ourselves to such a height
As that the stay
Of either may
Create the burden light.

And as this round
Is nowhere found
To flaw, or else to sever:
So let our love
As endless prove,
And pure as gold for ever.

—*Robert Herrick*

"Alas, 'tis true I have gone here and there"

Alas, 'tis true I have gone here and there
And made myself a motley to the view,
Gored mine own thoughts, sold cheap what is
    most dear,
Made old offenses of affections new.
Most true it is that I have looked on truth
Askance and strangely; but, by all above,
These blenches gave my heart another youth,
And worse essays proved thee my best of love.
Now all is done, have what shall have no end.
Mine appetite I never more will grind
On newer proof, to try an older friend,
A god in love, to whom I am confined.
    Then give me welcome, next my heaven the
        best,
    Even to thy pure and most loving breast.

—*William Shakespeare*

Romance

I will make you brooches and toys for your
　　delight
Of bird-song at morning and star-shine at
　　night.
I will make a palace fit for you and me
Of green days in forests and blue days at sea.

I will make my kitchen, and you shall keep your
　　room,
Where white flows the river and bright blows
　　the broom,
And you shall wash your linen and keep your
　　body white
In rainfall at morning and dewfall at night.

And this shall be for music when no one else is
   near,
The fine song for singing, the rare song to
   hear!
That only I remember, that only you admire,
Of the broad road that stretches and the
   roadside fire.

—Robert Louis Stevenson

The Oblation

Ask nothing more of me, sweet;
   All I can give you I give.
      Heart of my heart, were it more,
More would be laid at your feet—
   Love that should help you to live,
      Song that should spur you to soar.

All things were nothing to give,
   Once to have sense of you more,
      Touch you and taste of you, sweet,
Think you and breathe you and live,
   Swept of your wings as they soar,
      Trodden by chance of your feet.

I that have love and no more
   Give you but love of you, sweet.
      He that hath more, let him give;
He that hath wings, let him soar;
   Mine is the heart at your feet
      Here, that must love you to live.

—*Algernon Charles Swinburne*

A Line-Storm Song

The line-storm clouds fly tattered and swift,
  The road is forlorn all day,
Where a myriad snowy quartz stones lift,
  And the hoof-prints vanish away.
The roadside flowers, too wet for the bee,
  Expend their bloom in vain.
Come over the hills and far with me,
  And be my love in the rain.

The birds have less to say for themselves
  In the wood-world's torn despair
Than now these numberless years the elves,
  Although they are no less there:
All song of the woods is crushed like some
  Wild, easily shattered rose.
Come, be my love in the wet woods; come,
  Where the boughs rain when it blows.

There is the gale to urge behind
    And bruit our singing down,
And the shallow waters aflutter with wind
    From which to gather your gown.
What matter if we go clear to the west,
    And come not through dry-shod?
For wilding brooch shall wet your breast
    The rain-fresh goldenrod.

Oh, never this whelming east wind swells
    But it seems like the sea's return
To the ancient lands where it left the shells
    Before the age of the fern;
And it seems like the time when after doubt
    Our love came back amain.
Oh, come forth into the storm and rout
    And be my love in the rain.

—*Robert Frost*

Courtship

My Lesbia, let us live and love,
  Let crabbed Age talk what it will.
The Sun when down, returns above,
  But we, once dead, must be so still.

Kiss me a thousand times, and then
  Give me a hundred kisses more,
Now kiss a thousand times again,
  Then t'other hundred as before.

Come, a third thousand, and to those
  Another hundred kisses fix;
That done, to make the sweeter close,
  We'll millions of kisses mix.

And huddle them together so,
  That we ourselves shan't know how many,
And others can't their number know,
  If we should envy'd be by any.

And then, when we have done all this,
  That our pleasures may remain,
We'll continue on our bliss,
  By unkissing all again.

Thus we'll love, and thus we'll live,
  While our posting minutes fly,
We'll have no time to vex or grieve,
  But kiss and unkiss till we die.

—*Alexander Brome*

Summer

Come we to the summer, to the summer we will
    come,
For the woods are full of bluebells and the
    hedges full of bloom,
And the crow is on the oak a-building of her nest,
And love is burning diamonds in my true
    lover's breast;
She sits beneath the whitehorn a-plaiting of her
    hair,
And I will to my true lover with a fond request
    repair;
I will look upon her face, I will in her beauty
    rest,
And lay my aching weariness upon her lovely
    breast.

The clock-a-clay is creeping on the open bloom
   of May
The merry bee is trampling the pinky threads
   all day,
And the chaffinch it is brooding on its grey
   mossy nest
In the whitehorn bush where I will lean upon
   my lover's breast;
I'll lean upon her breast and I'll whisper in her
   ear
That I cannot get a wink o'sleep for thinking of
   my dear;
I hunger at my meat and I daily fade away
Like the hedge rose that is broken in the heat of
   the day.

—*John Clare*

Ruth

She stood breast high amid the corn,
Clasped by the golden light of morn,
Like the sweetheart of the sun,
Who many a glowing kiss had won.

On her cheek an autumn flush,
Deeply ripened;—such a blush
In the midst of brown was born,
Like red poppies grown with corn.

Round her eyes her tresses fell,
Which were blackest none could tell,
But long lashes veiled a light,
That had else been all too bright.

And her hat, with shady brim,
Made her tressy forehead dim;—
Thus she stood amid the stooks,
Praising God with sweetest looks:—

Sure, I said, heaven did not mean,
Where I reap thou shouldst but glean,
Lay thy sheaf adown and come,
Share my harvest and my home.

—*Thomas Hood*

"I dreamt the same old dream again"

I dreamt the same old dream again:
It was on a night in May,
We sat beneath the linden then,
Pledging eternal faith.

What swearing went on between us both,
Giggles, caresses no end;
To help me be mindful of my oath,
You bit me in the hand.

O sweetheart of the gazes bright!
O fair and mordant one!
The swearing was fine and right,
The biting was overdone.

—*Heinrich Heine (Translated by Walter Arndt)*

"I will give my love an apple without e'er a core"

I will give my love an apple without e'er a core,
I will give my love a house without e'er a door,
I will give my love a palace wherein she may be
And she may unlock it without e'er a key.

My head is the apple without e'er a core,
My mind is the house without e'er a door,
My heart is the palace wherein she may be
And she may unlock it without e'er a key

I will give my love a cherry without e'er a stone,
I will give my love a chick without e'er a bone,
I will give my love a ring, not a rent to be seen,
I will get my love children without any crying.

When the cherry's in blossom there's never no
  stone,
When the chick's in the womb there's never no
  bone,
And when they're rinning running not a rent to
  be seen,
And when they're child-making they're seldom
  crying.

—*Anonymous*

Meet Me in the Green Glen

Love, meet me in the green glen,
   Beside the tall elm-tree,
Where the sweetbriar smells so sweet agen;
   There come with me.
     Meet me in the green glen.

Meet me at the sunset
   Down in the green glen,
Where we've often met
   By hawthorn-tree and foxes' den,
     Meet me in the green glen.

Meet me in the green glen,
   By sweetbriar bushes there;
Meet me by your own sen,
   Where the wild thyme blossoms fair.
     Meet me in the green glen.

Meet me by the sweetbriar,
  By the mole-hill swelling there;
When the west glows like a fire
  God's crimson bed is there.
    Meet me in the green glen.

—*John Clare*

The Passionate Shepherd to His Love

Come live with me and be my love,
And we will all the pleasures prove
That valleys, groves, hills, and fields,
Woods, or steepy mountain yields.

And we will sit upon the rocks
Seeing the shepherds feed their flocks,
By shallow rivers, to whose falls
Melodious birds sing madrigals.

And I will make thee beds of roses
And a thousand fragrant posies,
A cap of flowers and a kirtle
Embroider'd all with leaves of myrtle.

A gown made of the finest wool,
Which from our pretty lambs we pull;
Fair linèd slippers for the cold,
With buckles of the purest gold.

A belt of straw and ivy buds,
With coral clasps and amber studs:
And if these pleasures may thee move,
Come live with me and be my love.

The shepherd swains shall dance and sing
For thy delight each May morning:
If these delights thy mind may move,
Then live with me and be my love.

—*Christopher Marlowe*

The Nymph's Reply to the Shepherd

If all the world and love were young,
And truth in every shepherd's tongue,
These pretty pleasures might me move
To live with thee and be thy love.

Time drives the flocks from field to fold,
When rivers rage and rocks grow cold,
And Philomel becometh dumb;
The rest complains of cares to come.

The flowers do fade, and wanton fields
To wayward winter reckoning yields:
A honey tongue, a heart of gall,
Is fancy's spring, but sorrow's fall.

Thy gowns, thy shoes, thy beds of roses,
Thy cap, thy kirtle, and thy posies
Soon break, soon wither, soon forgotten,
In folly ripe, in reason rotten.

Thy belt of straw and ivy buds,
Thy coral clasps and amber studs,
All these in me no means can move
To come to thee and be thy love.

But could youth last and love still breed,
Had joys no date nor age no need,
Then these delights my mind might move
To live with thee and be thy love.

—*Sir Walter Raleigh*

An Answer to Another Persuading a Lady to Marriage

Forbear, bold youth, all's Heaven here,
    And what you do aver,
To others, courtship may appear,
    'Tis sacriledge to her.

She is a publick deity,
    And were't not very odd
She should depose her self to be
    A pretty household god?

First make the sun in private shine,
    And bid the world adieu,
That so he may his beams confine
    In complement to you.

But if of that you do despair,
   Think how you did amiss,
To strive to fix her beams which are
   More bright and large than this.

—*Katherine Philips*

I Love You

I love your lips when they're wet with wine
   And red with a wild desire;
I love your eyes when the lovelight lies
   Lit with a passionate fire.
I love your arms when the warm white flesh
   Touches mine in a fond embrace;
I love your hair when the strands enmesh
   Your kisses against my face.

Not for me the cold, calm kiss
   Of a virgin's bloodless love;
Not for me the saint's white bliss,
   Nor the heart of a spotless dove.
But give me the love that so freely gives
   And laughs at the whole world's blame,
With your body so young and warm in my arms,
   It sets my poor heart aflame.

So kiss me sweet with your warm wet mouth,
    Still fragrant with ruby wine,
And say with a fervor born of the South
    That your body and soul are mine.
Clasp me close in your warm young arms,
    While the pale stars shine above,
And we'll live our whole young lives away
    In the joys of a living love.

—*Ella Wheeler Wilcox*

A Man's Requirements

I
Love me Sweet, with all thou art,
  Feeling, thinking, seeing;
Love me in the lightest part,
  Love me in full being.

II
Love me with thine open youth
  In its frank surrender;
With the vowing of thy mouth,
  With its silence tender.

III
Love me with thine azure eyes,
  Made for earnest granting;
Taking colour from the skies,
  Can Heaven's truth be wanting?

IV
Love me with their lids, that fall
　　Snow-like at first meeting;
Love me with thine heart, that all
　　Neighbours then see beating.

V
Love me with thine hand stretched out
　　Freely—open-minded:
Love me with thy loitering foot,—
　　Hearing one behind it.

VI
Love me with thy voice, that turns
　　Sudden faint above me;
Love me with thy blush that burns
　　When I murmur *Love me!*

VII

Love me with thy thinking soul,
  Break it to love-sighing;
Love me with thy thoughts roll
  On through living—dying.

VIII

Love me when in thy gorgeous airs,
  When the world has crowned thee;
Love me, kneeling at thy prayers,
  With the angels round thee.

IX

Love me pure, as musers do,
  Up the woodlands shady:
Love me gaily, fast and true,
  As a winsome lady.

X
Through all hopes that keep us brave,
    Farther off or nigher,
Love me for the house and grave,
    And for something higher.

XI
Thus, if thou wilt prove me, Dear,
    Woman's love no fable,
I will love *thee*—half a year—
    As a man is able.

—*Elizabeth Barrett Browning*

Loving in Truth

Loving in truth, and fain in verse my love to show,
That She, dear She, might take some pleasure of
  my pain;
Pleasure might cause her read, reading might
  make her know,
Knowledge might pity win, and pity grace
  obtain;
I sought fit words to paint the blackest face of
  woe,
Studying inventions fine, her wits to entertain
Oft turning others' leaves, to see if thence
  would flow
Some fresh and fruitful showers upon my
  sunburned brain.
But words came halting forth, wanting
  Invention's stay;
Invention, Nature's child, fled step-dame
  Study's blows;

And others' feet still seemed but strangers in
my way.
Thus, great with child to speak, and helpless in
my throes,
Biting my truant pen, beating myself for spite.
"Fool," said my Muse to me, "look in thy heart,
and write!"

—*Sir Philip Sidney*

SEDUCTION

An Argument

I've oft been told by learned friars,
   That wishing and the crime are one,
And Heaven punishes desires
   As much as if the deed were done.

If wishing damns us, you and I
   Are damned to all our heart's content;
Come, then, at least we may enjoy
   Some pleasure for our punishment!

—*Thomas Moore*

"Dear, why should you command me to my rest"

Dear, why should you command me to my rest,
When now the night doth summon all to sleep?
Methinks this time becometh lovers best;
Night was ordained together friends to keep.
How happy are all other living things,
Which though the day disjoin by sev'ral flight,
The quiet evening yet together brings,
And each returns unto his love at night!
O thou that art so courteous else to all,
Why shouldst thou, Night, abuse me only thus,
That ev'ry creature to his kind dost call,
And yet 'tis thou dost only sever us?
   Well could I wish it would be ever day,
    If when night comes you bid me go away.

—*Michael Drayton*

The Flea

Mark but this flea, and mark in this,
How little that which thou deny'st me is;
Me it sucked first, and now sucks thee,
And in this flea, our two bloods mingled be;
Confess it, this cannot be said
A sin, or shame, or loss of maidenhead,
    Yet this enjoys before it woo,
    And pampered swells with one blood made of
        two,
    And this, alas, is more than we would do.

Oh stay, three lives in one flea spare,
Where we almost, nay more than married are.
This flea is you and I, and this
Our marriage bed, and marriage temple is;
Though parents grudge, and you, we'are met,
And cloistered in these living walls of jet.

Though use make you apt to kill me,
Let not to this, self murder added be,
And sacrilege, three sins in killing three.
Cruel and sudden, hast thou since
Purpled thy nail, in blood of innocence?
In what could this flea guilty be,
Except in that drop which it sucked from thee?
Yet thou triumph'st, and say'st that thou
Find'st not thyself, nor me the weaker now;
'Tis true, then learn how false, fears be;
Just so much honour, when thou yield'st to
    me,
Will waste, as this flea's death took life from
    thee.

—*John Donne*

Love's Philosophy

The fountains mingle with the river,
  And the rivers with the ocean;
The winds of heaven mix forever,
  With a sweet emotion;
Nothing in the world is single;
  All things by a law divine
In one another's being mingle:—
  Why not I with thine?

See! the mountains kiss high heaven,
  And the waves clasp one another;
No sister flower would be forgiven
  If it disdained its brother;
And the sunlight clasps the earth,
  And the moonbeams kiss the sea:—
What are all these kissings worth,
  If thou kiss not me?

—*Percy Bysshe Shelley*

Come, Fill the Cup

Come, fill the cup, and in the fire of spring
Your winter garment of repentance fling.
The bird of time has but a little way
To flutter—and the bird is on the wing.

—*Omar Kháyyam*

Medicine Song of
an Indian Lover

I
Who, maiden, makes this river flow?
The Spirit—he makes its ripples glow—
But I have a charm that can make thee, dear,
Steal o'er the wave to thy lover here.

II
Who, maiden, makes this river flow?
The Spirit—he makes its ripples glow—
Yet every blush that my love would hide,
Is mirror'd for me in the tell-tale tide.

III
And though thou shouldst sleep on the
    farthest isle,
Round which these dimpling waters smile—
Yet I have a charm that can make thee, dear,
Steal over the wave to thy lover here.

—*Ojibwa*

To His Coy Mistress

Had we but world enough, and time,
This coyness, Lady, were no crime.
We would sit down and think which way
To walk and pass our long love's day.
Thou by the Indian Ganges' side
Shouldst rubies find: I by the tide
Of Humber would complain. I would
Love you ten years before the Flood,
And you should, if you please, refuse
Till the conversion of the Jews.
My vegetable love should grow
Vaster than empires, and more slow;
An hundred years should go to praise
Thine eyes and on thy forehead gaze;
Two hundred to adore each breast;
But thirty thousand to the rest;
An age at least to every part,
And the last age should show your heart;

For, Lady, you deserve this state,
Nor would I love at lower rate.
   But at my back I always hear
Time's wingèd chariot hurrying near;
And yonder all before us lie
Deserts of vast eternity.
Thy beauty shall no more be found,
Nor, in thy marble vault, shall sound
My echoing song: then worms shall try
That long preserved virginity,
And your quaint honour turn to dust,
And into ashes all my lust:
The grave's a fine and private place,
But none, I think, do there embrace.
   Now therefore, while the youthful hue

Sits on thy skin like morning dew,
And while thy willing soul transpires
At every pore with instant fires,
Now let us sport us while we may,
And now, like amorous birds of prey,
Rather at once our time devour
Than languish in his slow-chapt power.
Let us roll all our strength and all
Our sweetness up into one ball,
And tear our pleasures with rough strife
Thorough the iron gates of life:
Thus, though we cannot make our sun
Stand still, yet we will make him run.

—*Andrew Marvell*

"Sweet Cupid, ripen her desire"

Sweet Cupid, ripen her desire,
  Thy joyful harvest may begin;
If age approach a little nigher,
  'Twill be too late to get it in.

Cold winter storms lay standing corn,
  Which once too ripe will never rise,
And lovers wish themselves unborn,
  When all their joys lie in their eyes.

Then, sweet, let us embrace and kiss.
  Shall beauty shale upon the ground?
If age bereave us of this bliss,
  Then will no more such sport be found.

—*Anonymous*

"Go, lovely rose"

Go, lovely Rose—
    Tell her that wastes her time and me,
    That now she knows,
When I resemble her to thee,
How sweet and fair she seems to be.

    Tell her that's young,
And shuns to have her graces spied,
    That hadst thou sprung
In deserts where no men abide,
Thou must have uncommended died.

    Small is the worth
Of beauty from the light retired:
    Bid her come forth,
Suffer herself to be desired,
And not blush so to be admired

Then die—that she
The common fate of all things rare
    May read in thee;
How small a part of time they share
That are so wondrous sweet and fair!

—*Edmund Waller*

To Dianeme

Give me one kiss,
   And no more;
If so be, this
   Makes you poor,
To enrich you
   I'll restore
For that one, two
   Thousand score.

—*Robert Herrick*

"Think not of it, sweet one, so"

Think not of it, sweet one, so;
    Give it not a tear;
Sigh thou mayest, but bid it go
    Any, any where.

Do not look so sad, sweet one,
    Sad and fadingly:
Shed one drop then—It is gone—
    Oh! 'twas born to die.

Still so pale?—then, dearest, weep;
    Weep! I'll count the tears:
And each one shall be a bliss
    For thee in after years.

Brighter has it left thine eyes
    Than a sunny hill:
And thy whispering melodies
    Are tenderer still.

Yet, as all things mourn awhile
    At fleeting blisses,
Let us too!—but be our dirge
    A dirge of kisses.

—*John Keats*

The Kiss

"I saw you take his kiss!" "'Tis true."
    "O, modesty!" "'Twas strictly kept:
He thought me asleep; at least I knew
    He thought I thought he thought I slept."

—*Coventry Patmore*

"What guile is this, that those her golden tresses"

What guile is this, that those her golden tresses,
She doth attire under a net of gold;
And with sly skill so cunningly them dresses,
That which is gold or hair, may scarce be told?
Is it that men's frail eyes, which gaze too bold,
She may entangle in that golden snare;
And being caught may craftily enfold,
Their weaker hearts, which are not well aware?
Take heed therefore, mine eyes, how ye do stare
Henceforth too rashly on that guileful net,
In which if ever ye entrappèd are,
Out of her bands ye by no means shall get.
Fondness it were for any being free,
To covet fetters, though they golden be.

—*Edmund Spenser*

Delight in Disorder

A sweet disorder in the dress
Kindles in clothes a wantonness:
A lawn about the shoulders thrown
Into a fine distraction:
An erring lace which here and there
Enthralls the crimson stomacher:
A cuff neglectful, and thereby
Ribands to flow confusedly:
A winning wave (deserving note)
In the tempestuous petticoat:
A careless shoestring, in whose tie
I see a wild civility:
Do more bewitch me, than when art
Is too precise in every part.

—*Robert Herrick*

The Fair Singer

To make a final conquest of all me,
Love did compose so sweet an enemy,
In whom both beauties to my death agree,
Joining themselves in fatal harmony;
That while she with her eyes my heart does bind,
She with her voice might captivate my mind.

I could have fled from one but singly fair,
My disentangled soul itself might save,
Breaking the curled trammels of her hair.
But how should I avoid to be her slave,
Whose subtle art invisibly can wreath
My fetters of the very air I breathe?

It had been easy fighting in some plain,
Where victory might hang in equal choice,
But all resistance against her is vain,
Who has th'advantage both of eyes and voice,
And all my forces needs must be undone,
She having gained both the wind and sun.

—*Andrew Marvell*

Serpentine

In my dreams of love, I am a serpent!
gliding and undulating like a current,
my eyes, two pills of sleeplessness
and hypnosis; the tip of a spell
my tongue... I draw you in like a wail!
    I am a capsule abyss.

My body is a ribbon of excess,
gliding and undulating like a caress...

In my dreams of hatred, I am a serpent!
My tongue, a venomous vent;
my head lit by a diabolic crown,
the visage of death—fatal fade-away
through pupils; and my body, in gems drowned,
    the sheath of a flashing ray!

If so I dream my flesh, so is my mind, you see:
    a long, long body, serpentine,
vibrating eternal—voluptuously!

—*Delmira Augustini (Translated by Natalia Sucre)*

Why So Pale and Wan?

Why so pale and wan, fond lover?
  Prithee, why so pale?
Will, when looking well can't move her,
  Looking ill prevail?
  Prithee, why so pale?

Why so dull and mute, young sinner?
  Prithee, why so mute?
Will, when speaking well can't win her,
  Saying nothing do 't?
  Prithee, why so mute?

Quit, quit for shame! This will not move;
  This cannot take her.
If of herself she will not love,
  Nothing can make her:
  The devil take her!

—*Sir John Suckling*

WORSHIP AND
DEVOTION

"How do I love thee?
Let me count the ways"

How do I love thee? Let me count the ways.
I love thee to the depth and breadth and height
My soul can reach, when feeling out of sight
For the ends of Being and ideal Grace.
I love thee to the level of every day's
Most quiet need, by sun and candle-light.
I love thee freely, as men strive for Right;
I love thee purely, as they turn from Praise.
I love thee with the passion put to use
In my old griefs, and with my childhood's faith.
I love thee with a love I seemed to lose
With my lost saints—I love thee with the breath,
Smiles, tears, of all my life!—and, if God choose,
I shall but love thee better after death.

—*Elizabeth Barrett Browning*

from *Romeo and Juliet*

ROMEO: If I profane with my unworthiest hand
　　This holy shrine, the gentle sin is this;
　　My lips, two blushing pilgrims, ready
　　　　stand
　　To smooth that rough touch with a
　　　　tender kiss.
JULIET: Good pilgrim, you do wrong your hand
　　　　too much,
　　Which mannerly devotion shows in
　　　　this;
　　For saints have hands that pilgrims'
　　　　hands do touch,
　　And palm to palm is holy palmers' kiss.
ROMEO: Have not saints lips, and holy
　　　　palmers too?
JULIET: Ay, pilgrim, lips that they must use in
　　　　prayer.

ROMEO: O! then, dear saint, let lips do what hands do;
   They pray, Grant thou, lest faith turn to despair.
JULIET: Saints do not move, though grant for prayers' sake.
ROMEO: Then move not, while my prayers' effect I take.

—*William Shakespeare*

To Anthea, Who May Command Him Anything

Bid me to live, and I will live
   Thy protestant to be;
Or bid me love, and I will give
   A loving heart to thee.

A heart as soft, a heart as kind,
   A heart as sound and free,
As in the whole world thou canst find,
   That heart I'll give to thee.

Bid that heart stay, and it will stay,
   To honour thy decree;
Or bid it languish quite away,
   And 't shall do so for thee.

Bid me to weep, and I will weep,
    While I have eyes to see;
And having none, yet I will keep
    A heart to weep for thee.

Bid me despair, and I'll despair,
    Under that cypress tree;
Or bid me die, and I will dare
    E'en death, to die for thee.

Thou art my life, my love, my heart,
    The very eyes of me;
And hast command of every part,
    To live and die for thee.

—*Robert Herrick*

Song

How many times do I love thee, dear?
  Tell me how many thoughts there be
    In the atmosphere
    Of a new-fall'n year,
Whose white and sable hours appear
  The latest flake of Eternity:—
So many times do I love thee, dear.

How many times do I love again?
  Tell me how many beads there are
    In a silver chain
    Of evening rain,
Unravelled from the tumbling main,
  And threading the eye of a yellow star:—
So many times do I love again.

—Thomas Lovell Beddoes

To One That Asked Me Why I Loved S. G.

Why do I love? go ask the glorious sun
Why every day it round the world doth run:
Ask Thames and Tiber why they ebb and flow:
Ask damask roses why in June they blow:
Ask ice and hail the reason why they're cold:
Decaying beauties, why they will grow old:
They'll tell thee, Fate, that everything doth move,
Inforces them to this, and me to love.
There is no reason for our love or hate,
'Tis irresistible as Death or Fate;
'Tis not his face; I've sense enough to see,
That is not good, though doated on by me:
Nor is't his tongue, that has this conquest won,
For that at least is equalled by my own:

His carriage can to none obliging be,
'Tis rude, affected, full of vanity:
Strangely ill natur'd, peevish and unkind,
Unconstant, false, to jelousy inclin'd:
His temper could not have so great a power,
'Tis mutable, and changes every hour:
Those vigorous years that women so adore
Are past in him: he's twice my age and more;
And yet I love this false, this worthless man,
With all the passion that a woman can;
Doat on his imperfections, though I spy
Nothing to love; I love, and know not why.
Since 'tis decreed in the dark book of Fate,
That I should love, and he should be ingrate.

—*Ephelia*

A Red, Red Rose

O my luve is like a red, red rose,
  That's newly sprung in June.
O my luve is like the melodie
  That's sweetly played in tune.

As fair art thou, my bonnie lass,
  So deep in luve am I;
And I will luve thee still, my dear,
  Till a' the seas gang dry.

Till a' the seas gang dry, my dear,
  And the rocks melt wi' the sun!
And I will love thee still, my dear.
  While the sands o' life shall run.

And fare thee weel, my only luve,
  And fare thee weel awhile!
And I will come again, my luve,
  Though it were ten thousand mile!

—*Robert Burns*

A Song: When June Is Past, the Fading Rose

Ask me no more where Jove bestows,
When June is past, the fading rose;
For in your beauty's orient deep
These flowers as in their causes, sleep.

Ask me no more whither doth stray
The golden atoms of the day;
For in pure love heaven did prepare
Those powders to enrich your hair.

Ask me no more whither doth haste
The nightingale, when May is past;
For in your sweet dividing throat
She winters and keeps warm her note.

Ask me no more where those stars' light
That downwards fall in dead of night;
For in your eyes they sit, and there,
Fixèd become, as in their sphere.

Ask me no more if east or west
The phoenix builds her spicy nest;
For unto you at last she flies,
And in your fragrant bosom dies.

—*Thomas Carew*

She Walks in Beauty

She walks in beauty, like the night
Of cloudless climes and starry skies;
And all that's best of dark and bright
Meet in her aspect and her eyes;
Thus mellow'd to that tender light
Which heaven to gaudy day denies.

One shade the more, one ray the less,
Had half impair'd the nameless grace
Which waves in every raven tress,
Or softly lightens o'er her face;
Where thoughts serenely sweet express
How pure, how dear their dwelling-place.

And on that cheek, and o'er that brow,
So soft, so calm, yet eloquent,
The smiles that win, the tints that glow,
But tell of days in goodness spent,
A mind at peace with all below,
A heart whose love is innocent!

—*George Gordon, Lord Byron*

The Beloved

It is enough of honor for one lifetime
  To have known you better than the rest have
    known,
The shadows and the colors of your voice,
  Your will, immutable and still as stone.

The shy heart, so lonely and so gay,
  The sad laughter and the pride of pride,
The tenderness, the depth of tenderness
  Rich as the earth, and wide as heaven is wide.

—*Sara Teasdale*

"She was a Phantom of delight"

She was a Phantom of delight
When first she gleamed upon my sight;
A lovely Apparition, sent
To be a moment's ornament;
Her eyes as stars of Twilight fair;
Like Twilight's, too, her dusky hair;
But all things else about her drawn
From May-time and the cheerful Dawn;
A dancing Shape, an Image gay,
To haunt, to startle, and way-lay.

I saw her upon nearer view,
A Spirit, yet a Woman too!
Her household motions light and free,
And steps of virgin-liberty;
A countenance in which did meet
Sweet records, promises as sweet;
A Creature not too bright or good
For human nature's daily food;
For transient sorrows, simple wiles,
Praise, blame, love, kisses, tears, and smiles.

And now I see with eye serene
The very pulse of the machine;
A Being breathing thoughtful breath,
A Traveller between life and death;
The reason firm, the temperate will,
Endurance, foresight, strength, and
 skill;
A perfect Woman, nobly planned,
To warn, to comfort, and command;
And yet a Spirit still, and bright
With something of angelic light.

—*William Wordsworth*

Her Face

Her face
so fair
first bent
mine eye

Her tongue
so sweet
then drew
mine ear

Her wit
so sharp
then hit
my heart

Mine eye
to like
her face
doth lead

Mine ear
to learn
her tongue
doth teach

My heart
to love
her wit
doth move

Her face
with beams
doth blind
mine eye

Her tongue
with sound
doth charm
mine ear

Her wit
with art
doth knit
my heart

Mine eye
with life
her face
doth feed

Mine ear
with hope
her tongue
doth feast

My heart
with skill
her wit
doth fill

O face
with frowns
wrong not
mine eye

O tongue
with checks
vex not
mine ear

O wit
with smart
wound not
my heart

This eye
shall joy
her face
to serve

This ear
shall yield
her tongue
to trust

This heart
shall swear
her wit
to fear.

—*Arthur Gorges*

The Ideal

Never those beauties in old prints vignetted,
Those shopworn products of a worthless age,
With slippered feet and fingers castanetted,
The thirst of hearts like my heart can assuage.

To Gavarni, the poet of chloroses,
I leave his troupe of beauties sick and wan;
I cannot find among those pale, pale roses,
The red ideal mine eyes would gaze upon.

You, Lady Macbeth, a soul strong in crime,
Aeschylus' dream born in a northern clime—
Ah, you could quench my dark heart's deep
    desiring;

Or you, Michelangelo's daughter, Night,
In a strange posture dreamily admiring
Your beauty fashioned for a giant's delight!

—*Charles Baudelaire (Translated by F. P. Sturm)*

"Sapphires are those eyes of yours"

Sapphires are those eyes of yours,
Ravishingly sweet,
Oh, triply fortunate the man
Whom lovingly they greet.

Your heart is like the diamond
That sparkles noble beams;
Oh, triply lucky is the man
For whom with love it gleams.

Your lips are like twin ruby stones,
None lovelier anywhere;
Oh, triply fortunate the man
To whom they love aver.

Oh, if I knew this lucky man
And found him thus in clover,
just a tête-à-tête in the deep green wood,
His luck would soon be over.

—*Heinrich Heine (Translated by Walter Arndt)*

"In what bright realm, what sphere of radiant thought"

In what bright realm, what sphere of radiant
   thought
Did Nature find the model whence she drew
That delicate dazzling image where we view
Here on this earth what she in heaven wrought?
What fountain-haunting nymph, what dryad,
   sought
In groves, such golden tresses ever threw
Upon the gust? What heart such virtues knew?—
Though her chief virtue with my death is fraught.
He looks in vain for heavenly beauty, he
Who never looked upon her perfect eyes,
The vivid blue orbs turning brilliantly—
He does not know how Love yields and denies;
He only knows, who knows how sweetly she
Can talk and laugh, the sweetness of her sighs.

—*Francesco Petrarca (Translated by Joseph Auslander)*

To Citriodora

I turn and see you passing in the street
When you are not. I take another way,
Lest missing you the fragrance of the day
Exhale, and I know not that it is sweet.
And marking you I follow, and when we meet
Love laughs to see how sudden I am gay;
Sweetens the air with fragrance like a spray
Of sweet verbena, and bids my heart to beat.

Love laughs; and girls that take you by the hand,
Know that a sweet thing has befallen them;
And women give their hearts into your heart.
There is, I think, no man in all the land
But would be glad to touch your garment's hem.
And I, I love you with a love apart.

—*Philip Henry Savage*

Carmen 43

Hail, although of nose not neat,
Black of eyes nor trim of feet,
Long of fingers, dry of mouth,
Nor too dainty-tongued, forsooth,
Mistress of no better man
Than a bankrupt Formian.
Does your province not declare you
Beautiful? and even compare you
With my Lesbia? O disgraced
Age, incapable of taste!

—*Catullus (Translated by Arthur Symons)*

A Praise of His Love

Give place, ye lovers, here before
That spent your boasts and brags it vain;
My lady's beauty passeth more
The best of yours, I dare well sayn,
Than doth the sun the candle-light,
Or brightest day the darkest night.

And thereto hath a troth as just
As had Penelope the fair;
For what she saith, ye may it trust,
As it by writing sealèd were;
And virtues hath she many mo
Than I with pen have skill to show.

I could rehearse, if that I wold,
The whole effect of Nature's plaint,
When she had lost the perfit mould,
The like to whom she could not paint;
With wringing hands, how she did cry,
And what she said, I know it, I.

I know she swore with raging mind,
Her kingdom only set apart,
There was no loss by law of kind,
That could have gone so near her heart;
And this was chiefly all her pain;
She could not make the like again.

Sith Nature thus gave her the praise,
To be the chiefest work she wrought;
In faith, methink, some better ways
On your behalf might well be sought,
Than to compare, as ye have done,
To match the candle with the sun.

—*Henry Howard, Earl of Surrey*

"My mistress' eyes are nothing like the sun"

My mistress' eyes are nothing like the sun;
Coral is far more red than her lips' red:
If snow be white, why then her breasts are dun;
If hairs be wires, black wires grow on her head.
I have seen roses damasked, red and white,
But no such roses see I in her cheeks;
And in some perfumes is there more delight
Than in the breath that from my mistress reeks.
I love to hear her speak, yet well I know
That music hath a far more pleasing sound:
I grant I never saw a goddess go,—
My mistress, when she walks, treads on the
 ground.
  And yet, by heaven, I think my love as rare
  As any she belied with false compare.

—*William Shakespeare*

When You Are Old

When you are old and grey and full of sleep,
And nodding by the fire, take down this book,
And slowly read, and dream of the soft look
Your eyes had once, and of their shadows deep;

How many loved your moments of glad grace,
And loved your beauty with love false or true,
But one man loved the pilgrim soul in you,
And loved the sorrows of your changing face;

And bending down beside the glowing bars
Murmur, a little sadly, how Love fled
And paced upon the mountains overhead
And hid his face amid a crowd of stars.

—*W. B. Yeats*

DISCORD

Carmen 92
To Lesbia From Catullus, Jul. 18th 1736

Lesbia for ever on me rails;
   To talk on me she never fails:
Yet, hang me, but for all her Art;
   I find that I have gain'd her Heart:
My proof is this: I plainly see
   The Case is just the same with me:
I curse her ev'ry hour sincerely;
   Yet, hang me, but I love her dearly.

—*Catullus (Translated by Jonathan Swift)*

A Song from *An Evening's Love*

DAMON   Celimena, of my heart,
               None shall e'er bereave you:
               If, with your good leave, I may
               Quarrel with you once a day,
               I will never leave you.

CELIMENA Passion's but an empty name
               Where respect is wanting:
               Damon you mistake your ayme;
               Hang your heart, and burn your flame,
               If you must be ranting.

DAMON   Love as dull and muddy is,
               As decaying liquor:
               Anger sets it on the lees,
               And refines it by degrees,
               Till workes it quicker.

CELIMENA   Love by quarrels to beget
Wisely you endeavour;
With a grave Physician's wit
Who to cure an Ague fit
Put me in a Feavor.

DAMON   Anger rouzes love to fight,
And his only bayt is,
'Tis the spurre to dull delight,
And is but an eager bite,
When desire at height is.

CELIMENA   If such drops of heat can fall
In our wooing weather;
If such drops of heat can fall,
We shall have the Devil and all
When we come together.

—*John Dryden*

The Indifferent

I can love both fair and brown,
Her whom abundance melts, and her whom want
    betrays,
Her who loves loneness best, and her who masks
    and plays,
    Her whom the country formed, and whom the
    town,
      Her who believes, and her who tries,
      Her who still weeps with spongy eyes,
    And her who is dry cork, and never cries;
    I can love her, and her, and you and you,
    I can love any, so she be not true.

    Will no other vice content you?
Will it not serve your turn to do, as did your
    mothers?
Or have you old vices spent, and now would
    find out others?
    Or doth a fear, that men are true, torment you?

Oh we are not, be not you so,
　　Let me, and do you, twenty know.
　Rob me, but bind me not, and let me go.
　Must I, who came to travail thorough you,
　Grow your fixed subject, because you are true?

　　Venus heard me sigh this song,
And by Love's sweetest part, variety, she swore,
She heard not this till now; and and't should be
　　so no more
　She went, examined, and returned ere long,
　　And said, alas, Some two or three
　　Poor heretics in love there be,
　Which think to 'stablish dangerous constancy.
　But I have told them, since you will be true,
　You shall be true to them, who are false to you.

—*John Donne*

The Variety

Thou sai'st I swore I lov'd thee best,
   And that my heart liv'd in thy breast;
   And now thou wondrest much that I
Should what I swore then, much deny,
And upon this thou taxest me
With faithlessnesse, inconstancy:
   Thou hast no reason so to do,
   Who can't dissemble ne'r must wooe.

That so I lov'd thee 'tis confest,
But 'twas because I judg'd thee best,
For then I thought that thou alone
Wast vertue's, beautie's paragon:
But now that the deceit I find,
To love thee still were to be blind;
   And I must needs confess to thee
   I love in love variety.

Alas! should I love thee alone,
In a short time I should love none;
Who on one well-lov'd feeds, yet,
Once being cloy'd, of all, loaths it;
Would'st thou be subject to a fate
To make me change my love to hate?
  Blame me not then, since 'tis for love
  Of thee, that I inconstant prove.

And yet in truth 'tis constancy,
For which I am accus'd by thee;
To nature those inconstant are,
Who fix their love on one that's faire;
Why did she, but for our delight,
Present such numbers to our sight?
  'Mongst all earthly kings, there's none
  Contented with one Crown alone.

—*John Dancer*

My Dear and Only Love

My dear and only Love, I pray
   This noble world of thee
Be govern'd by no other sway
   But purest monarchy;
For if confusion have a part,
   Which virtuous souls abhor,
And hold a synod in thy heart,
   I'll never love thee more.

Like Alexander I will reign,
   And I will reign alone,
My thoughts shall evermore disdain
   A rival on my throne.
He either fears his fate too much,
   Or his deserts are small,
That puts it not unto the touch
   To win or lose it all.

But I must rule and govern still,
    And always give the law,
And have each subject at my will,
    And all to stand in awe.
But 'gainst my battery, if I find
    Thou shunn'st the prize so sore
As thou sett'st me up a blind,
    I'll never love thee more.

Or in the empire of thy heart
    Where I should solely be,
Another do pretend a part
    And dares to vie with me;
Or if committees thou erect,
    And go on such a score,
I'll sing and laugh at thy neglect,
    And never love thee more.

But if thou wilt be constant then,
    And faithful of thy word,
I'll make thee glorious by my pen
    And famous by my sword;
I'll serve thee in such noble ways
    Was never heard before;
I'll crown and deck thee all with bays,
    And love thee evermore.

—*James Graham, Marquis of Montrose*

Neglect Returned

1

Proud *Strephon*! doe not think my Heart
So absolute a Slave:
Nor in so mean a servile state,
But if I say that you're Ingrate,
I've Pride, and Pow'r, enough, my Chains to
   Brave.

2

I Scorn to Grieve, or Sigh for one,
That does my Tears Neglect;
If in your Looks you Coldness wear,
Or a desire of Change Appear,
I can your Vows, your Love, and you Reject.

3

What refin'd Madness wou'd it be,
With Tears to dim those Eyes,
Whose Rays, if Grief do not Rebate,
Each hour new Lovers might Create,
And with each Look, gain a more glorious Prize!

4

Then do not think with Frowns to Fright,
Or Threaten me with Hate,
For I can be as cold as you,
Disdain as much, as proudly too,
And break my Chain in spight of Love or Fate.

—*Ephelia*

"Love still a boy, and oft a wanton is"

Love still a boy, and oft a wanton is,
    Schooled only by his mother's tender eye;
    What wonder then if he his lesson miss,
    When for so soft a rod dear play he try?
And yet my Star, because a sugared kiss
    In sport I sucked, while she asleep did lie,
    Doth lower, nay, chide; nay, threat for only this:
    Sweet, it was saucy Love, not humble I.
But no scuse serves, she makes her wrath appear
    In Beauty's throne, see now who dares come near
    Those scarlet judges, threatening bloody pain?
O heavenly fool, thy most kiss-worthy face,
    Anger invests with such a lovely grace,
    That Anger's self I needs must kiss again.

—*Sir Philip Sidney*

"No more be grieved at that which thou hast done"

No more be grieved at that which thou hast done:
Roses have thorns, and silver fountains mud,
Clouds and eclipses stain both moon and sun,
And loathsome canker lives in sweetest bud.
All men make faults, and even I in this,
Authorizing thy trespass with compare,
Myself corrupting, salving thy amiss,
Excusing thy sins more than thy sins are;
For to thy sensual fault I bring in sense—
Thy adverse party is thy advocate—
And 'gainst myself a lawful plea commence.
Such civil war is in my love and hate
  That I an accessory needs must be
  To that sweet thief which sorely robs from me.

—*William Shakespeare*

Vivien's Song

'In Love, if Love be Love, if Love be ours,
Faith and unfaith can ne'er be equal powers:
Unfaith in aught is want of faith in all.

'It is the little rift within the lute,
That by and by will make the music mute,
And ever widening slowly silence all.

'The little rift within the lover's lute
Or little pitted speck in garnered fruit,
That rotting inward slowly moulders all.

'It is not worth the keeping: let it go:
But shall it? answer, darling, answer, no.
And trust me not at all or all in all'.

—*Alfred, Lord Tennyson*

Tears Are Tongues

When Julia chid I stood as mute the while
As is the fish or tongueless crocodile.
Air coin'd to words, my *Julia* could not hear,
But she could see each eye to stamp a tear;
By which my angry mistress might descry
Tears are the noble language of the eye.
And when true love of words is destitute
The eyes by tears speak, while the tongue is mute.

—*Robert Herrick*

from *Modern Love*

Yet it was plain she struggled, and that salt
Of righteous feeling made her pitiful.
Poor twisting worm, so queenly beautiful!
Where came the cleft between us? whose the
    fault?
My tears are on thee, that have rarely dropped
As balm for any bitter wound of mine:
My breast will open for thee at a sign!
But, no: we are two reed pipes, coarsely stopped:
The God once filled them with his mellow breath;
And they were music till he flung them down,
Used! used! Hear now the discord-loving clown
Puff his gross spirit in them, worse than death!
I do not know myself without thee more:
In this unholy battle I grow base:
If the same soul be under the same face,
Speak, and a taste of that old time restore!

—*George Meredith*

Mortal Combat

It is because you were my friend,
    I fought you as the devil fights.
Whatever fortune God may send,
    For once I set the world to rights.

And that was when I thrust you down,
    And stabbed you twice and twice again,
Because you dared take off your crown,
    And be a man like other men.

—*Mary Coleridge*

The Division

Rain on the windows, creaking doors,
  With blasts that besom the green,
And I am here, and you are there,
  And a hundred miles between!

O were it but the weather, Dear,
  O were it but the miles
That summed up all our severance,
  There might be room for smiles.

But that thwart thing betwixt us twain,
  Which nothing cleaves or clears,
Is more than distance, Dear, or rain,
  And longer than the years!

—*Thomas Hardy*

Wed

For these white arms about my neck—
   For the dainty room, with its ordered grace—
For my snowy linen without a fleck—
   For the tender charm of this uplift face—

For the softened light and the homelike air—
   The low luxurious cannel fire—
The padded ease of my chosen chair—
   The devoted love that discounts desire—

I sometimes think, when Twelve is struck
   By the clock on the mantel, tinkling clear,
I would take—and thank the gods for the luck—
   One single hour with the boys and the beer.

Where the sawdust scent of a cheap saloon
   Is mingled with malt; where each man smokes,
Where they sing the street songs out of tune,
   Talk Art, and bandy ephemeral jokes.

By Jove, I do! And all the time
   I know not a man that is there to-night
But would barter his brains to be where I'm—
   And I'm well aware that the beggars are right.

—*Henry Cuyler Bunner*

A Woman's Last Word

Let's contend no more, Love,
   Strive nor weep:
All be as before, Love,
   —Only sleep!

What so wild as words are?
   I and thou
In debate, as birds are,
   Hawk on bough!

See the creature stalking
   While we speak!
Hush and hide the talking,
   Cheek on cheek!

What so false as truth is,
   False to thee?
Where the serpent's tooth is,
   Shun the tree—

Where the apple reddens
   Never pry—
Lest we lose our Edens
   Eve and I.

Be a god and hold me
   With a charm!
Be a man and fold me
   With thine arm!

Teach me, only teach, Love!
   As I ought.
I will speak thy speech, Love,
   Think thy thought—

Meet, if thou require it,
   Both demands,
Laying flesh and spirit
   In thy hands.

That shall be tomorrow,
  Not tonight;
I must bury sorrow
  Out of sight:

—Must a little weep, Love,
  (Foolish me!)
And so fall asleep, Love,
  Loved by thee.

—*Robert Browning*

Love, Maybe

Always
in the middle
of our bloodiest battles
you lay down your arms
like flowering mines

to conqueror me home.

—*Audre Lorde*

COMMUNION

My True-Love Hath My Heart, and I Have His

My true-love hath my heart, and I have his,
By just exchange one for another given:
I hold his dear, and mine he cannot miss,
There never was a better bargain driven:

My true-love hath my heart, and I have his,
My heart in me keeps him and me in one,
My heart in him his thoughts and senses guide:
He loves my heart, for once it was his own,
I cherish his because in me it bides:

My true-love hath my heart, and I have his.

—*Sir Philip Sidney*

To My Dear and Loving Husband

If ever two were one, then surely we.
If ever man were loved by wife, then thee;
If ever wife was happy in a man,
Compare with me, ye women, if you can.
I prize thy love more than whole mines of gold,
Or all the riches that the East doth hold.
My love is such that rivers cannot quench,
Nor aught but love from thee give recompense.
Thy love is such I can no way repay;
The heavens reward thee manifold, I pray.
Then while we live, in love let's so persevere,
That when we live no more, we may live ever.

—*Anne Bradstreet*

The Good Morrow

I wonder by my troth, what thou and I
   Did, till we loved? Were we not weaned till
     then?
But sucked on country pleasures, childishly?
   Or snorted we i'the seven sleepers' den?
'Twas so; But this, all pleasures fancies be.
If ever any beauty I did see,
Which I desired, and got, 'twas but a dream of
     thee.

And now good morrow to our waking souls,
   Which watch not one another out of fear;
For love, all love of other sights controls,
   And makes one little room, an everywhere.
Let sea-discoverers to new worlds have gone,
Let maps to others, worlds on worlds have
     shown,
Let us possess our world, each hath one, and is
     one.

My face in thine eye, thine in mine appears,
  And true plain hearts do in the faces rest,
Where can we find two better hemispheres
  Without sharp North, without declining West?
Whatever dies, was not mixed equally;
  If our two loves be one, or, thou and I
Love so alike, that none do slacken, none can die.

—*John Donne*

The Definition of Love

My love is of a birth as rare
As 'tis for object strange and high;
It was begotten by Despair
Upon Impossibility.

Magnanimous Despair alone
Could show me so divine a thing
Where feeble Hope could ne'er have flown,
But vainly flapp'd its tinsel wing.

And yet quickly might arrive
Where my extended soul is fixt,
But Fate does iron wedges drive,
And always crowds itself betwixt.

For Fate with jealous eye does see
Two perfect loves, nor lets them close;
Their union would her ruin be,
And her tyrannic pow'r depose.

And therefore her decrees of steel
Us as the distant poles have plac'd,
(Though love's whole world on us doth wheel)
Not by themselves to be embrac'd;

Unless the giddy heaven fall,
And earth some new convulsion tear;
And, us to join, the world should all
Be cramp'd into a planisphere.

As lines, so loves oblique may well
Themselves in every angle greet;
But ours so truly parallel,
Though infinite, can never meet.

Therefore the love which us doth bind,
But Fate so enviously debars,
Is the conjunction of the mind,
And opposition of the stars.

—*Andrew Marvell*

Heart's Haven

Sometimes she is a child within my arms,
Cowering beneath dark wings that love must
  chase,—
With still tears showering and averted face,
Inexplicably filled with faint alarms:
And oft from mine own spirit's hurtling
  harms
I crave the refuge of her deep embrace,—
Against all ills the fortified strong place
And sweet reserve of sovereign counter-
  charms.
And Love, our light at night and shade at
  noon,
Lulls us to rest with songs, and turns away
All shafts of shelterless tumultuous day.
Like the moon's growth, his face gleams
  through his tune;
And as soft waters warble to the moon,
Our answering spirits chime one roundelay.

—*Dante Gabriel Rossetti*

"Go from me"

Go from me. Yet I feel that I shall stand
Henceforward in thy shadow. Nevermore
Alone upon the threshold of my door
Of individual life, I shall command
The uses of my soul, nor lift my hand
Serenely in the sunshine as before,
Without the sense of that which I forbore—
Thy touch upon the palm. The widest land
Doom takes to part us, leaves thy heart in mine
With pulses that beat double. What I do
And what I dream include thee, as the wine
Must taste of its own grapes. And when I sue
God for myself, He hears that name of thine,
And sees within my eyes the tears of two.

—*Elizabeth Barrett Browning*

"In this world"

In this world,
love has no color—
yet how deeply
my body
is stained by yours.

—*Izumi Shikibu*

Monna Inominata, 4

I loved you first: but afterwards your love,
  Outsoaring mine, sang such a loftier song
As drowned the friendly cooings of my dove.
  Which owes the other most? My love was
    long,
  And yours one moment seemed to wax more
    strong;
I loved and guessed at you, you construed me
And loved me for what might or might not be—
  Nay, weights and measures do us both a wrong.
For verily love knows not "mine" or "thine";
With separate "I" and "thou" free love has done,
  For one is both and both are one in love:
Rich love knows nought of "thine that is not
    mine";
    Both have the strength and both the length
      thereof,
Both of us, of the love which makes us one.

—*Christina Rossetti*

Translation

We trekked into a far country,
My friend and I.
Our deeper content was never spoken,
But each knew all the other said.
He told me how calm his soul was laid
By the lack of anvil and strife.
"The wooing kestrel," I said, "mutes his mating-
  note
To please the harmony of this sweet silence."
And when at the day's end
We laid tired bodies 'gainst
The loose warm sands,
And the air fleeced its particles for a coverlet;
When star after star came out
To guard their lovers in oblivion—
My soul so leapt that my evening prayer
Stole my morning song!

—*Anne Spencer*

To Asra

Are there two things, of all which men possess,
That are so like each other and so near,
As mutual Love seems like to Happiness?
Dear Asra, woman beyond utterance dear!
This Love which ever welling at my heart,
Now in its living fount doth heave and fall,
Now overflowing pours thro' every part
Of all my frame, and fills and changes all,
Like vernal waters springing up through snow,
This Love that seeming great beyond the power
Of growth, yet seemeth ever more to grow,
Could I transmute the whole to one rich Dower
Of Happy Life, and give it all to Thee,
Thy lot, methinks, were Heaven, thy age,
    Eternity!

—*Samuel Taylor Coleridge*

Wedding Prayer

Now you will feel no rain,
　For each of you will be shelter to the other.
Now you will feel no cold,
　For each of you will be warmth to the other.
Now there is no more loneliness,
　For each of you will be companion to the
　　other.
Now you are two bodies,
　But there is only one life before you.
Go now to your dwelling place
　To enter into the days of your togetherness
And may your days be good and long upon the
　　earth.

—*Traditional Apache Prayer*

The Mystery

Your eyes drink of me,
   Love makes them shine,
Your eyes that lean
   So close to mine.

We have long been lovers,
   We know the range
Of each other's moods
   And how they change;

But when we look
   At each other so
Then we feel
   How little we know;

The spirit eludes us,
   Timid and free—
Can I ever know you
   Or you know me?

—*Sara Teasdale*

"There's a sacred limit
to any closeness"

There's a sacred limit to any closeness,
Even the passionate fact can't transcend,
Though in fearful silence lips on lips may press
And the heart love tears to pieces won't mend.

And friendship is powerless and years
Of intense high-minded happiness,
Where the soul is free, a stranger to fears
Of the slow languors of passionate excess.

Those who strive to reach it play the part
Of madness, those who succeed are stricken—
  And
Now you understand why my heart
Is not beating beneath your hand.

—*Anna Akhmatova (Translated by Lyn Coffin)*

Meeting at Night

I
The grey sea and the long black land;
And the yellow half-moon large and low;
And the startled little waves that leap
In fiery ringlets from their sleep,
As I gain the cove with pushing prow,
And quench its speed i' the slushy sand.

II
Then a mile of warm sea-scented beach;
Three fields to cross till a farm appears;
A tap at the pane, the quick sharp scratch
And blue spurt of a lighted match,
And a voice less loud, thro' its joys and fears,
Than the two hearts beating each to each!

—*Robert Browning*

The Lover's Death

We will have voluptuous couches, full of subtle,
    faint, perfume,
We will have soft clasping cushions, deep and
    silent as the tomb;
Strange flowers on the window ledges, shutting
    out the azure skies,
Tingeing all the sunlight's languor with
    a thousand crimson dyes.

Using, slowly, as if grudging, their consuming,
    final heat,
Our two hearts will meet together, as two
    mighty flames might meet,
And reflect their double splendour, and their
    double streams of light;
In your soul and mine, my darling,
    as on mirrors burnish'd bright.

On an evening, rosy tinted, and with mystic
    blue half-dark,
Our two hearts will throb together, and
    exchange their dying spark,
Like a long-drawn sighing, sobbing, overladen
    with 'farewells'.

Later on will come an angel, floating thro' the
    open door,
Joyful in his task of mercy, mighty with death-
    conquering spells,
To revive the tarnish'd mirrors, and the
    shatter'd flames once more!

—*Charles Baudelaire (Translated by Henry Curwen)*

"We two, how long
we were fool'd"

We two, how long we were fool'd,
Now transmuted, we swiftly escape as Nature
    escapes,
We are Nature, long have we been absent, but
    now we return,
We become plants, trunks, foliage, roots, bark,
We are bedded in the ground, we are rocks,
We are oaks, we grow in the openings side by side,
We browse, we are two among the wild herds
    spontaneous as any,
We are two fishes swimming in the sea together,
We are what locust blossoms are, we drop scent
    around lanes mornings and evenings,
We are also the coarse smut of beasts,
    vegetables, minerals,

We are two predatory hawks, we soar above
and look down,
We are two resplendent suns, we it is who
balance ourselves orbic and stellar, we are as
two comets,
We prowl fang'd and four-footed in the woods,
we spring on prey,
We are two clouds forenoons and afternoons
driving overhead,
We are seas mingling, we are two of those
cheerful waves rolling over each other and
interwetting each other,
We are what the atmosphere is, transparent,
receptive, pervious, impervious,
We are snow, rain, cold, darkness, we are each
product and influence of the globe,

We have circled and circled till we have arrived
    home again, we two,
We have voided all but freedom and all but our
    own joy.

—*Walt Whitman*

TORMENT

On His Own Love

I hate and love—ask why—I can't explain;
I feel 'tis so, and feel it racking pain.

—*George Lamb*

"Love uses me as a target
for his lance"

Love uses me as a target for his lance,
As snow in sunlight or as wax in flame,
Or wind-swept cloud; and though upon your
  name
I call, O Laura, pity looks askance.
Your flashing eyes first caused the dart to dance
In my sick breast; nor time nor place can tame
Its fire. From you, that take no thought of blame,
Were born the pangs that thwart deliverance.
Each thought drives arrows, and your face a sun,
My passion's heat: and these Love urges well
To rend my heart, to dazzle me to hell.
Your song celestial and your speech soft-spun
And your dear breathings of such strong control—
These build the sweet storm that destroys my
  soul.

—*Francesco Petrarca (Translated by Joseph Auslander)*

"I find no peace and all my war is done"

I find no peace and all my war is done.
I fear and hope, I burn and freeze like ice.
I fly above the wind yet can I not arise.
And naught I have and all the world I seize on.
That looseth nor locketh, holdeth me in prison
And holdeth me not, yet can I scape no wise;
Nor letteth me live nor die at my device
And yet of death it giveth me occasion.
Without eyen I see and without tongue I plain.
I desire to perish and yet I ask health.
I love another and thus I hate myself.
I feed me in sorrow and laugh in all my pain.
Likewise displeaseth me both death and life,
And my delight is causer of this strife.

—*Sir Thomas Wyatt*

"If one would see how Love has mastered me"

If one would see how Love has mastered me,
How he assails and conquers with his art,
How, now with fire, now ice, he plagues my
   heart,
How he seeks glory from my misery;

If one would see beau's yearning agony
For belle, who naught but torment will impart,
Read on: here will he see the sting, the smart,
That God and Goddess mine deal recklessly.

Well will he learn that Love, unreasoning,
Is a sweet woe, a lovely prisoning,
A gust of wind that feeds our hope in vain:

Well will he learn that man is much beguiled—
Indeed, benighted—when he lets a child,
And one unsighted, as his master reign.

—*Pierre de Ronsard (Translated by Norman Shapiro)*

"When love, puffed up with rage of high disdain"

When love, puffed up with rage of high disdain,
Resolved to make me pattern of his might,
Like foe, whose wits inclined to deadly spite,
Would often kill, to breed more feeling pain;
He would not, armed with beauty, only reign
On those affects which easily yield to sight,
But virtue sets so high, that reason's light,
For all his strife, can only bondage gain:
So that I live to pay a mortal fee,
Dead-palsy-sick of all my chiefest parts;
Like those whom dreams make ugly monsters
   see,
And can cry 'Help!' with nought but groans and
   starts.
   Longing to have, having no wit to wish,
   To starving minds such is god Cupid's dish.

—*Sir Phillip Sidney*

Love is a Sickness

Love is a sickness full of woes,
   All remedies refusing;
A plant that with most cutting grows,
   Most barren with best using.
      Why so?

More we enjoy it, more it dies;
If not enjoy'd, it sighing cries—
      Heigh ho!

Love is a torment of the mind,
   A tempest everlasting;
And Jove hath made it of a kind
   Not well, nor full nor fasting.
      Why so?

More we enjoy it, more it dies;
If not enjoy'd, it sighing cries—
      Heigh ho!

—*Samuel Daniel*

In which she describes rationally the irrational effects of love

    That my heart is suffering
from love pangs is plain,
but less clear by far
is the cause of its pain.
    To make fancy come true
my poor heart strains
but, thwarting desire,
only gloom remains.
    And when most I plead
and lament my plight,
though I see my sadness,
its cause escapes sight.
    I yearn for the chance
to which I aspire,
yet when it impends,

I shrink from desire,
   lest, sensing at hand
that longed-for day,
my misgivings spoil it,
fear drive it away.
   And if, reassured,
I clasp it tight,
with the slightest pretext,
all pleasure takes flight.
   My timid misgivings
turn boon into bane
and for love's very sake,
I must show disdain!

—*Sister Juana Inés de la Cruz*
(Translated by Alan Trueblood)

On Monsieur's Departure

I grieve and do not show my discontent,
I love and yet am forced to seem to hate,
I do, yet dare not say I ever meant,
I seem stark mute but inwardly do prate.
   I am and not, I freeze and yet am burned,
   Since from myself another self I turned.

My care is like my shadow in the sun,
Follows me flying, flies when I pursue it,
Stands and lies by me, doth what I have done.
His too familiar care doth make me rue it.
   No means I find to rid him from my breast,
   Till by the end of things it be supprest.

Some gentler passion slide into my mind,
For I am soft and made of melting snow;
Or be more cruel, love, and so be kind.
Let me or float or sink, be high or low.
   Or let me live with some more sweet content.
   Or die and so forget what love ere meant.

—*Elizabeth I*

"Alas! so all things now do hold their peace"

Alas! so all things now do hold their peace,
Heaven and earth disturbéd in no thing;
The beasts, the air, the birds their song do cease,
The nightés chare the stars about doth bring.
Calm is the sea, the waves work less and less;
So am not I, whom love, alas, doth wring,
Bringing before my face the great increase
Of my desires, whereat I weep and sing,
In joy and woe, as in a doubtful case.
For my sweet thoughts sometime do pleasure
   bring,
But by and by the cause of my disease
Gives me a pang that inwardly doth sting,
When that I think what grief it is again
To live and lack the thing should rid my pain.

—*Henry Howard, Earl of Surrey*

Mediocrity in Love Rejected

Give me more love, or more disdain;
  The torrid or the frozen zone
Bring equal ease unto my pain;
  The temperate affords me none:
Either extreme, of love or hate,
Is sweeter than a calm estate.

Give me a storm; if it be love,
  Like Danaë in that golden shower,
I swim in pleasure; if it prove
  Disdain, that torrent will devour
My vulture hopes; and he's possessed
Of heaven that's but from hell released.
  Then crown my joys, or cure my pain;
  Give me more love or more disdain.

—*Thomas Carew*

A Match

If love were what the rose is,
   And I were like the leaf,
Our lives would grow together
In sad or singing weather,
Blown fields or flowerful closes,
   Green pleasure or gray grief;
If love were what the rose is,
   And I were like the leaf.

If I were what the words are,
   And love were like the tune,
With double sound and single
Delight our lips would mingle,
With kisses glad as birds are
   That get sweet rain at noon;
If I were what the words are,
   And love were like the tune.

If you were life, my darling,
   And I your love were death,
We'd shine and snow together
Ere March made sweet the weather
With daffodil and starling
   And hours of fruitful breath;
If you were life, my darling,
   And I your love were death.

If you were thrall to sorrow,
   And I were page to joy,
We'd play for lives and seasons
With loving looks and treasons
And tears of night and morrow
   And laughs of maid and boy;
If you were thrall to sorrow,
   And I were page to joy.

If you were April's lady,
   And I were lord in May,
We'd throw with leaves for hours
And draw for days with flowers,
Till day like night were shady
   And night were bright like day:
If you were April's lady,
   And I were lord in May.

If you were queen of pleasure,
   And I were king of pain,
We'd hunt down love together,
Pluck out his flying feather,
And teach his feet a measure,
   And find his mouth a rein;
If you were queen of pleasure,
   And I were king of pain.

—*Algernon Charles Swinburne*

Spring

When daisies pied and violets blue,
   And lady-smocks all silver-white,
And cuckoo-buds of yellow hue
   Do paint the meadows with delight,
The cuckoo then, on every tree,
Mocks married men; for thus sings he,
        "Cuckoo!
Cuckoo, cuckoo!" O word of fear,
Unpleasing to a married ear!

When shepherds pipe on oaten straws,
   And merry larks are ploughmen's clocks,
When turtles tread, and rooks, and daws,
   And maidens bleach their summer smocks,
The cuckoo then, on every tree,
Mocks married men; for thus sings he,
        "Cuckoo!
Cuckoo, cuckoo!" O word of fear,
Unpleasing to a married ear!

—*William Shakespeare*

"Peer of gods he seemeth to me"

I
Peer of gods he seemeth to me, the blissful
Man who sits and gazes at thee before him,
Close beside thee sits, and in silence hears thee
      Silverly speaking,

II
Laughing Love's low laughter. Oh this, this only
Stirs the troubled heart in my breast to tremble.
For should I but see thee a little moment,
      Straight is my voice hushed;

III
Yea, my tongue is broken, and through and
   through me
'Neath the flesh, impalpable fire runs tingling;
Nothing see mine eyes, and a noise of roaring
   Waves in my ears sounds;

IV

Sweat runs down in rivers, a tremor seizes
All my limbs and paler than grass in autumn,
Caught by pains of menacing death I falter,
    Lost in the love trance.

—*Sappho (Translated by J. A. Symonds)*

The Change or Miracle

What Miracles this childish God has wrought!
Things strange above belief! who wou'd have
  thought
My temper cou'd be to this Tameness brought?

I, who the wanton Boy so long defi'd,
And his Fantastick Godhead did deride,
And laugh'd at Lovers with insulting Pride:

Now pale and faint, beneath his Altar lie,
Own him a great and glorious Deity,
And want the pitty that I did deny.

For my proud Victor does my Tears neglect,
Smiles at my Sighs, treats me with disrespect,
And if I do complain, with frowns I'm check't.

Though all I sue for, be the empty bliss
Of a kind Look, or at the most a Kiss,
Yet he's so cruel to deny me this.

Before my Passion struck my Reason blind,
Such Generosity dwelt in my mind,
I car'd for none, and yet to all was kind.

But now I tamely bend, and sue in vain,
To one that takes delight t' encrease my pain,
And proudly does Me, and my Love disdain.

—*Ephelia*

The Triple Fool

I am two fools, I know,
For loving, and for saying so
    In whining poetry;
But where's that wiseman, that would not be I,
    If she would not deny?
Then as th'earth's inward narrow crooked lanes
Do purge sea water's fretful salt away,
    I thought, if I could draw my pains
Through rhyme's vexation, I should them allay.
Grief brought to numbers cannot be so fierce,
For, he tames it, that fetters it in verse.

    But when I have done so,
Some man, his art and voice to show,
    Doth set and sing my pain,
And, by delighting many, frees again
    Grief, which verse did restrain.

To love and grief tribute of verse belongs,
But not of such as pleases when 'tis read,
   Both are increased by such songs:
For both their triumphs so are published,
And I, which was two fools, do so grow three;
Who are a little wise, the best fools be.

—*John Donne*

"Th' expense of spirit in a waste of shame"

Th' expense of spirit in a waste of shame
Is lust in action; and, till action, lust
Is perjured, murd'rous, bloody, full of blame,
Savage, extreme, rude, cruel, not to trust;
Enjoyed no sooner but despisèd straight;
Past reason hunted, and no sooner had,
Past reason hated as a swallowed bait
On purpose laid to make the taker mad;
Made in pursuit, and in possession so;
Had, having, and in quest to have, extreme;
A bliss in proof, and proved, a very woe,
Before, a joy proposed; behind, a dream.
  All this the world well knows, yet none
    knows well
  To shun the heaven that leads men to this hell.

—*William Shakespeare*

ABSENCE AND
SEPARATION

A Valediction: forbidding Mourning

As virtuous men pass mildly away,
    And whisper to their souls, to go,
Whilst some of their sad friends do say,
    The breath goes now, and some say, no:

So let us melt, and make no noise,
    No tear-floods, nor sigh-tempests move,
'Twere profanation of our joys
    To tell the laity our love.

Moving of th' earth brings harms and fears,
    Men reckon what it did and meant,
But trepidation of the spheres,
    Though greater far, is innocent.

Dull sublunary lovers' love
    (Whose soul is sense) cannot admit
Absence, because it doth remove
    Those things which elemented it.

But we by a love, so much refined,
　　That our selves know not what it is,
Inter-assured of the mind,
　　Care less, eyes, lips, and hands to miss.

Our two souls therefore, which are one,
　　Though I must go, endure not yet
A breach, but an expansion,
　　Like gold to aery thinness beat.

If they be two, they are two so
　　As stiff twin compasses are two,
Thy soul the fixed foot, makes no show
　　To move, but doth, if th'other do.

—*John Donne*

"Sweetest love
return again"

Sweetest love return again,
    Make not too long stay
Killing mirth and forcing pain,
    Sorrow leading way:
Let us not thus parted be,
Love and absence ne'er agree.

But since you must needs depart,
    And me hapless leave,
In your journey take my heart,
    Which will not deceive:
Yours it is, to you it flies,
Joying in those loved eyes.

So in part we shall not part,
   Though we absent be;
Time nor place nor greatest smart
   Shall my bands make free:
Tied I am, yet think it gain;
In such knots I feel no pain.

But can I live, having lost
   Chiefest part of me?
Heart is fled, and sight is crossed:
   These my fortunes be.
Yet dear heart go, soon return:
As good there, as here to burn.

—*Mary Wroth*

A Farewell

With all my will, but much against my heart,
We two now part.
My Very Dear,
Our solace is, the sad road lies so clear.
It needs no art,
With faint, averted feet
And many a tear,
In our opposed paths to persevere.
Go thou to East, I West.
We will not say
There's any hope, it is so far away.
But, O, my Best,
When the one darling of our widowhead,
The nursling Grief,
Is dead,
And no dews blur our eyes
To see the peach-bloom come in evening skies,

Perchance we may,
Where now this night is day,
And even through faith of still averted feet,
Making full circle of our banishment,
Amazed meet;
The bitter journey to the bourne so sweet
Seasoning the termless feast of our content
With tears of recognition never dry.

—*Coventry Patmore*

First farewell to S. G.

Farewell my dearer half, joy of my heart,
Heaven only knows how loth I am to part:
Whole Months but hours seem, when you are
   here,
When absent, every Minute is a Year:
Might I but always see thy charming Face,
I'de live on Racks, and with no easier place.
But we must part, your Interest says we must;
Fate, me no longer with such Treasure trust.
I wou'd not tax you with Inconstancy,
Yet *Strephon*, you are not so kind as I:
No Interest, no nor Fate it felt has pow'r
To tempt me from the Idol I adore:
But since you needs will go, may *Africk* be
Kinder to you, than *Europe* is to me:
May all you meet and every thing you view
Give you such Transport as I met in you.
May no sad thoughts disturb your quiet mind,
Except you'l think of her you left behind.

—*Ephelia*

Aubade

Stay, O sweet, and do not rise,
The light that shines comes from thine eyes;
The day breaks not, it is my heart,
Because that you and I must part.
    Stay, or else my joys will die,
    And perish in their infancy.

—*Anonymous*

A Letter to Daphnis, April 2nd 1685

This to the Crown, and blessing of my life,
The much lov'd husband, of a happy wife.
To him, whose constant passion found the art
To win a stubborn, and ungrateful heart;
And to the World, by tend'rest proof discovers
They err, who say that husbands can't be lovers.
With such return of passion, as is due,
Daphnis I love, Daphnis my thoughts persue,
Daphnis, my hopes, my joys, are bounded all in
    you:
Ev'n I, for Daphnis, and my promise sake,
What I in women censure, undertake.
But this from love, not vanity, proceeds;
You know who writes; and I who 'tis that reads.
Judge not my passion, by my want of skill,
Many love well, though they express itt ill;
And I your censure cou'd with pleasure bear,
Wou'd you but soon return, and speak itt here.

—*Anne Finch, Countess of Winchilsea*

Westron Wynde

Westron wynde when wyll thow blow
the smalle rayne downe can rayne
Chryst yf my love wer in my armys
and I yn my bed agayne

—*Anonymous*

After Parting

Oh I have sown my love so wide
That he will find it everywhere;
It will awake him in the night,
It will enfold him in the air.

I set my shadow in his sight
And I have winged it with desire,
That it may be a cloud by day
And in the night a shaft of fire.

—*Sara Teasdale*

"If the dull substance of my flesh were thought"

If the dull substance of my flesh were thought,
Injurious distance should not stop my way,
For then despite of space I would be brought,
From limits far remote, where thou dost stay.
No matter then although my foot did stand
Upon the farthest earth removed from thee;
For nimble thought can jump both sea and land,
As soon as think the place where he would be.
But, ah, thought kills me that I am not thought,
To leap large lengths of miles when thou art gone,
But that so much of earth and water wrought,
I must attend time's leisure with my moan,
   Receiving naught by elements so slow
   But heavy tears, badges of either's woe.

—*William Shakespeare*

When, Dearest, I But Think On Thee

   When, dearest, I but think on thee,
Methinks all things that lovely be
Are present, and my soul delighted:
   For beauties that from worth arise
   Are like the grace of deities,
Still present with us, though unsighted.

   Thus while I sit and sigh the day
With all his spreading lights away,
Till night's black wings do overtake me:
   Thinking on thee, thy beauties then,
   As sudden lights do sleeping men,
So they by their bright rays awake me.

Thus absence dies, and dying proves
No absence can consist with loves
That do partake of fair perfection:
  Since in the darkest night they may
  By their quick motion find a way
To see each other by reflection.

The waving sea can with such flood
Bathe some high palace that hath stood
Far from the main up in the river:
  Oh think not then but love can do
  As much, for that's an ocean too,
That flows not every day, but ever.

—*Owen Felltham*

To Mary

I sleep with thee, and wake with thee,
And yet thou art not there;
I fill my arms with thoughts of thee,
And press the common air.
Thy eyes are gazing upon mine
When thou art out of sight;
My lips are always touching thine
At morning, noon, and night.

I think and speak of other things
To keep my mind at rest,
But still to thee my memory clings
Like love in woman's breast.
I hide it from the world's wide eye
And think and speak contrary,
But soft the wind comes from the sky
And whispers tales of Mary.

The night-wind whispers in my ear,
The moon shines on my face;
The burden still of chilling fear
I find in every place.
The breeze is whispering in the bush,
And the leaves fall from the tree,
All sighing on, and will not hush,
Some pleasant tales of thee.

—*John Clare*

Concentration

A hut green-shadowed among firs,—
A sun that slopes in amber air,—
Lone wandering, my head I bare,
While some far thrush the silence stirs.

No flocks of wild geese thither fly,
And she—ah! she is far away;
Yet all my thoughts behold her stay,
As in the golden hours gone by.

The clouds scarce dim the water's sheen,
The moon-bathed islands wanly show,
And sweet words falter to and fro—
Though the great River rolls between.

—*Ssu-K'ung T'u*
(Translated by L. Cranmer-Byng)

The Bliss of Absence

Drink, oh youth, joy's purest ray
From thy loved one's eyes all day,

And her image paint at night!
Better rule no lover knows,
Yet true rapture greater grows,

When far sever'd from her sight.

Powers eternal, distance, time,
Like the might of stars sublime,

Gently rock the blood to rest,
O'er my senses softness steals,
Yet my bosom lighter feels,

And I daily am more blest.

Though I can forget her ne'er,
Yet my mind is free from care,

I can calmly live and move;
Unperceived infatuation
Longing turns to adoration,

Turns to reverence my love.

Ne'er can cloud, however light,
Float in ether's regions bright,

When drawn upwards by the sun,
As my heart in rapturous calm.
Free from envy and alarm,

Ever love I her alone!

—*Johann Wolfgang von Goethe*
(Translated by Edgar Alfred Bowring)

The End of the Episode

Indulge no more may we
In this sweet-bitter pastime:
The love-light shines the last time
  Between you, Dear, and me.

There shall remain no trace
Of what so closely tied us,
And blank as ere love eyed us
  Will be our meeting-place.

The flowers and thymy air,
Will they now miss our coming?
The dumbles thin their humming
  To find we haunt not there?

Though fervent was our vow,
Though ruddily ran our pleasure,
Bliss has fulfilled its measure,
  And sees its sentence now.

Ache deep; but make no moans:
Smile out; but stilly suffer:
The paths of love are rougher
   Than thoroughfares of stones.

—*Thomas Hardy*

"So we'll go no more a-roving"

So, we'll go no more a-roving
   So late into the night,
Though the heart be still as loving
   And the moon be still as bright.

For the sword outwears its sheath,
   And the soul wears out the breast,
And the heart must pause to breathe,
   And love itself have rest.

Though the night was made for loving,
   And the day returns too soon,
Yet we'll go no more a-roving
   By the light of the moon.

—*George Gordon, Lord Byron*

The Lost Mistress

All's over, then: does truth sound bitter
   As one at first believes?
Hark, 'tis the sparrows' good-night twitter
   About your cottage eaves!

And the leaf-buds on the vine are woolly,
   I noticed that, today;
One day more bursts them open fully
   —You know the red turns grey.

Tomorrow we meet the same then, dearest?
   May I take your hand in mine?
Mere friends are we,—well, friends the merest
   Keep much that I resign:

For each glance of the eye so bright and black,
  Though I keep with heart's endeavour,—
Your voice, when you wish the snowdrops back,
  Though it stay in my soul for ever!—

Yet I will but say what mere friends say,
  Or only a thought stronger;
I will hold your hand but as long as all may,
  Or so very little longer!

—*Robert Browning*

A Valediction

If we must part,
   Then let it be like this;
Not heart on heart,
   Nor with the useless anguish of a kiss;
But touch mine hand and say:
"Until tomorrow or some other day,
   If we must part."

Words are so weak
   When love hath been so strong:
Let silence speak:
   "Life is a little while, and love is long;
A time to sow and reap,
And after harvest a long time to sleep,
   But words are weak."

—*Ernest Dowson*

HOPE

Sudden Light

I have been here before,
　　But when or how I cannot tell:
I know the grass beyond the door,
　　The sweet keen smell,
The sighing sound, the lights around the shore.

You have been mine before,—
　　How long ago I may not know:
But just when at the swallow's soar
　　Your neck turn'd so,
Some veil did fall,—I knew it all of yore.

Has this been thus before?
　　And shall not thus time's eddying flight
Still with our lives our love restore
　　In death's despite,
And day and night yield one delight once more?

—*Dante Gabriel Rossetti*

First Love

I ne'er was struck before that hour
  With love so sudden and so sweet,
Her face it bloomed like a sweet flower
  And stole my heart away complete.
My face turned pale as deadly pale.
  My legs refused to walk away,
And when she looked, what could I ail?
  My life and all seemed turned to clay.

And then my blood rushed to my face
  And took my eyesight quite away,
The trees and bushes round the place
  Seemed midnight at noonday.
I could not see a single thing,
  Words from my eyes did start—
They spoke as chords do from the string,
  And blood burnt round my heart.

Are flowers the winter's choice?
   Is love's bed always snow?
She seemed to hear my silent voice,
   Not love's appeals to know.
I never saw so sweet a face
   As that I stood before.
My heart has left its dwelling-place
   And can return no more.

—*John Clare*

To My Excellent Lucasia,
on Our Friendship

I did not live until this time
   Crown'd my felicity,
When I could say without a crime,
   I am not thine, but Thee.

This carcase breath'd, and walkt, and slept,
   So that the World believ'd
There was a soul the motions kept:
   But they were all deceiv'd.

For as a watch by art is wound
   To motion, such was mine:
But never had Orinda found
   A soul till she found thine;

Which now inspires, cures and supplies,
    And guides my darkened breast:
For thou art all that I can prize,
    My Joy, my life, my Rest.

No bridegroom's nor crown-conqueror's mirth
    To mine compar'd can be:
They have but pieces of this Earth,
    I've all the World in thee.

Then let our flames still light and shine,
    And no false fear control,
As innocent as our design,
    Immortal as our soul.

—*Katherine Philips*

"I used to wander aimlessly"

I used to wander aimlessly,
Wanton my goal, grievous my plight.
You dear hands led me, guided me.

Over the far horizon, night
Glowed with the pallid hope of dawn.
Your eyes' glance was my morning light.

No sound—save his own tread upon
The ground—to ease the wanderer's heart,
Your voice encouraged me: "Go on!"

Yes, my heart—dark, cowed, set apart,
Alone—bewailed its dire distress.
Sweet love, with its all-conquering art,

Joined us as one in joyousness.

—*Paul Verlaine (Translated by Norman R. Shapiro)*

Eulalie

    I dwelt alone
    In a world of moan,
        And my soul was a stagnant tide,
Till the fair and gentle Eulalie became my
    blushing bride—
Till the yellow-haired young Eulalie became my
    smiling bride.

    Ah, less—less bright
    The stars of night
        Than the eyes of the radiant girl!

    And never a flake
    That the vapor can make
        With the moon-tints of purple and pearl,
Can vie with the modest Eulalie's most
    unregarded curl—
Can compare with the bright-eyed Eulalie's
    most humble and careless curl.

Now doubt—now Pain
Come never again,
   For her soul gives me sigh for sigh,
And all day long
Shines, bright and strong,
   Astarté within the sky,
While ever to her dear Eulalie upturns her
  matron eye—
While ever to her young Eulalie upturns her
  violet eye.

—*Edgar Allan Poe*

"If I were loved, as I desire to be"

If I were loved, as I desire to be,
What is there in the great sphere of the earth,
And range of evil between death and birth,
That I should fear,—if I were loved by thee?
All the inner, all the outer world of pain
Clear love would pierce and cleave, if thou wert
   mine,
As I have heard that, somewhere in the main,
Fresh-water springs come up with bitter brine.
'Twere joy, not fear, clasped hand in hand with
   thee,
To wait for death—mute—careless of all ills,
Apart upon a mountain, though the surge
Of some new deluge from a thousand hills
Flung leagues of roaring foam into the gorge
Below us, as far on as eye could see.

—*Alfred, Lord Tennyson*

O Nightingale

O Nightingale, that on yon bloomy spray
   Warblest at eve, when all the woods are still,
   Thou with fresh hope the lover's heart dost fill,
While the jolly hours lead on propitious May.
Thy liquid notes that close the eye of day
   First heard before the shallow cuccoo's bill,
   Portend success in love; O if Jove's will
Have link'd that amorous power to thy soft lay,
   Now timely sing, ere the rude bird of hate
Foretel my hopeless doom in some grove nigh,
   As thou from year to year hast sung too late
For my relief, yet hadst no reason why:
   Whether the Muse or Love call thee his mate,
Both them I serve, and of their train am I.

—*John Milton*

"Most sweet it is with unuplifted eyes"

Most sweet it is with unuplifted eyes
To pace the ground, if path be there or none,
While a fair region round the traveller lies
Which he forbears again to look upon;
Pleased rather with some soft ideal scene,
The work of Fancy, or some happy tone
Of meditation, slipping in between
The beauty coming and the beauty gone.
If Thought and Love desert us, from that day
Let us break off all commerce with the Muse:
With Thought and Love companions of our way,
Whate'er the senses take or may refuse,
The Mind's internal heaven shall shed her dews
Of inspiration on the humblest lay.

—*William Wordsworth*

"'Hope' is the thing with feathers"

"Hope" is the thing with feathers—
That perches in the soul—
And sings the tune without the words—
And never stops —at all—

And sweetest—in the Gale—is heard—
And sore must be the storm—
That could abash the little Bird
That kept so many warm—

I've heard it in the chillest land—
And on the strangest Sea—
Yet, never, in Extremity,
It asked a crumb—of Me.

—*Emily Dickinson*

"You smiled, you spoke, and I believed"

You smiled, you spoke, and I believed,
By every word and smile deceived.
Another man would hope no more;
Nor hope I what I hoped before:
But let not this last wish be vain;
Deceive, deceive me once again!

—*Walter Savage Landor*

"Since there's no help"

Since there's no help, come let us kiss and part—
Nay, I have done, you get no more of me;
And I am glad, yea, glad with all my heart,
That thus so cleanly I myself can free.
Shake hands for ever, cancel all our vows,
And when we meet at any time again,
Be it not seen in either of our brows
That we one jot of former love retain.
Now at the last gasp of Love's latest breath,
When, his pulse failing, Passion speechless lies,
When Faith is kneeling by his bed of death,
And Innocence is closing up his eyes—
   Now if thou would'st, when all have given
      him over,
   From death to life thou might'st him yet
      recover.

—*Michael Drayton*

To Celia

Drink to me only with thine eyes,
   And I will pledge with mine;
Or leave a kiss but in the cup
   And I'll not look for wine.
The thirst that from the soul doth rise
   Doth ask a drink divine;
But might I of Jove's nectar sup,
   I would not change for thine.

I sent thee late a rosy wreath,
   Not so much honouring thee
As giving it a hope that there
   It could not withered be;
But thou thereon didst only breathe,
   And sent'st it back to me;
Since when it grows, and smells, I swear,
   Not of itself but thee!

—*Ben Jonson*

You'll Love Me Yet

You'll love me yet!—and I can tarry
   Your love's protracted growing:
June rear'd that bunch of flowers you carry,
   From seeds of April's sowing.

I plant a heartful now: some seed
   At least is sure to strike,
And yield—what you'll not pluck indeed,
   Not love, but, may be, like.

You'll look at least on love's remains,
   A grave's one violet:
Your look?—that pays a thousand pains.
   What's death? You'll love me yet!

—*Robert Browning*

"Those lips that Love's own hand did make"

Those lips that Love's own hand did make
Breath'd forth the sound that said "I hate"
To me that languish'd for her sake;
But when she saw my woeful state,
Straight in her heart did mercy come,
Chiding that tongue that, ever sweet,
Was us'd in giving gentle doom,
And taught it thus anew to greet:
"I hate" she alter'd with an end
That follow'd it as gentle day
Doth follow night, who like a fiend
From heaven to hell is flown away:
  "I hate" from hate away she threw,
  And sav'd my life, saying "not you."

—*William Shakespeare*

An Hour with Thee

An hour with thee! When earliest day
Dapples with gold the eastern grey,
Oh, what can frame my mind to bear
The toil and turmoil, cark and care,
New griefs, which coming hours unfold,
And sad remembrance of the old?
   One hour with thee.

One hour with thee! When burning June
Waves his red flag at pitch of noon;
What shall repay the faithful swain,
His labour on the sultry plain;
And, more than cave or sheltering bough,
Cool feverish blood and throbbing brow?
   One hour with thee.

One hour with thee! When sun is set,
Oh, what can teach me to forget
The thankless labours of the day;
The hopes, the wishes, flung away;
The increasing wants, and lessening gains,
The master's pride, who scorns my pains?
  One hour with thee.

—*Sir Walter Scott*

Love's Springtide

My heart was winter-bound until
   I heard you sing;
O voice of Love, hush not, but fill
   My life with Spring!

My hopes were homeless things before
   I saw your eyes;
O smile of Love, close not the door
   To paradise!

My dreams were bitter once, and then
   I found them bliss;
O lips of Love, give me again
   Your rose to kiss!

Springtide of Love! The secret sweet
   Is ours alone;
O heart of Love, at last you beat
   Against my own!

—*Frank Dempster Sherman*

I Love You

I love you for what you are, but I
   love you
yet more for what you are going to
   be.
I love you not so much for your
   realities
as for your ideals.
I pray for your desires that they may
   be great,
rather than for your satisfactions,
which may be so hazardously little.
You are going forward toward
   something great.
I am on the way with you,
and therefore I love you.

—*Carl Sandburg*

A Vision of Spring in Winter

O tender time that love thinks long to see,
   Sweet foot of spring that with her footfall sows
   Late snowlike flowery leavings of the snows,
Be not too long irresolute to be;
O mother-month, where have they hidden thee?
   Out of the pale time of the flowerless rose
I reach my heart out toward the springtime lands.
   I stretch my spirit forth to the fair hours,
     The purplest of the prime;
I lean my soul down over them, with hands
   Made wide to take the ghostly growths of
      flowers;
    I send my love back to the lonely time.

—*Algernon Charles Swinburne*

BITTERNESS

"They that have pow'r
to hurt and will do none"

They that have pow'r to hurt and will do
   none,
That do not do the thing they most do show,
Who, moving others, are themselves as stone,
Unmovèd, cold, and to temptation slow:
They rightly do inherit heaven's graces,
And husband nature's riches from expense,
They are the lords and owners of their faces,
Others but stewards of their excellence:
The summer's flow'r is to the summer sweet,
Though to itself it only live and die,
But if that flow'r with base infection meet,
The basest weed outbraves his dignity:
   For sweetest things turn sourest by their
     deeds,
   Lilies that fester smell far worse than weeds.

—*William Shakespeare*

The Message

Send home my long strayed eyes to me,
Which (oh) too long have dwelt on thee,
Yet since there they have learned such ill,
    Such forced fashions,
    And false passions,
      That they be
      Made by thee
Fit for no good sight, keep them still.

Send home my harmless heart again,
Which no unworthy thought could stain,
But if it be taught by thine
    To make jestings
    Of protestings,
      And cross both
      Word and oath,
Keep it, for then 'tis none of mine.

Yet send me back my heart and eyes,
That I may know, and see thy lies,
And may laugh and joy, when thou
    Art in anguish
    And dost languish
      For some one
      That will none,
Or prove as false as thou art now.

—*John Donne*

Song (Love Arm'd)

Love in fantastic triumph sat
  Whilst bleeding hearts around him flow'd,
For whom fresh paines he did create,
  And strange tyrannic power he show'd;

From thy bright eyes he took his fire,
  Which round about in sport he hurl'd;
But 'twas from mine he took desire,
  Enough to undo the amorous world.

From me he took his sighs and tears,
  From thee his pride and cruelty;
From me his languishments and fears,
  And every killing dart from thee.

Thus thou and I the god have arm'd,
  And set him up a deity;
But my poor heart alone is harm'd,
  Whilst thine the victor is, and free.

—*Aphra Behn*

The Grave of Love

I dug, beneath the cypress shade,
  What well might seem an elfin's grave;
And every pledge in earth I laid,
  That erst thy false affection gave.

I press'd them down the sod beneath;
  I placed one mossy stone above;
And twined the rose's fading wreath
  Around the sepulchre of love.

Frail as thy love, the flowers were dead
  Ere yet the evening sun was set:
But years shall see the cypress spread,
  Immutable as my regret.

—*Thomas Love Peacock*

"Envenomed are my songs"

Envenomed are my songs,
How could it be otherwise, tell?
Since you trickled poison
Into my life's clear well.

Envenomed are my songs,
How could it be otherwise, tell?
My heart holds many serpents,
And you, my love, as well.

—*Heinrich Heine*
(Translated by Walter Arndt)

"I abide and abide and better abide"

I abide and abide and better abide,
And after the old proverb, the happy day.
And ever my lady to me doth say,
'Let me alone and I will provide.'
I abide and abide and tarry the tide
And, with abiding, speed well ye may.
Thus do I abide, I wot, alway,
Neither obtaining nor yet denied.
Aye me, this long abiding
Seemeth to me, as who saith,
A prolonging of a dying death
Or a refusing of a desired thing.
Much were it better for to be plain
Than to say 'Abide' and yet shall not obtain.

—*Sir Thomas Wyatt*

"Fair ye be sure, but cruel and unkind"

Fair ye be sure, but cruel and unkind,
As is a tiger, that with greediness
Hunts after blood; when he by chance doth find
A feeble beast, doth felly him oppress.
Fair be ye sure, but proud and pitiless,
As is a storm, that all things doth prostrate;
Finding a tree alone all comfortless,
Beats on it strongly, it to ruinate.
Fair be ye sure, but hard and obstinate,
As is a rock amidst the raging floods:
'Gainst which, a ship, of succor desolate,
Doth suffer wreck both of herself and goods.
   That ship, that tree, and that same beast, am I,
    Whom ye do wreck, do ruin, and destroy.

—*Edmund Spenser*

This Lady's Cruelty

With how sad steps, O moon, thou climb'st the
   skies!
How silently, and with how wan a face!
What! May it be that even in heavenly place
That busy archer his sharp arrows tries?
Sure, if that long-with-love-acquainted eyes
Can judge of love, thou feel'st a lover's case:
I read it in thy looks; thy languished grace
To me, that feel the like, thy state descries.
Then, even of fellowship, O Moon, tell me,
Is constant love deemed there but want of wit?
Are beauties there as proud as here they be?
Do they above love to be loved, and yet
   Those lovers scorn whom that love doth
      possess?
   Do they call "virtue" there—ungratefulness?

—*Sir Philip Sidney*

Hatred

I shall hate you
Like a dart of stinging steel
Shot through still air
At even-tide.
Or solemnly
As pines are sober
When they stand etched
Against the sky.
Hating you shall be a game
Played with cool hands
And slim fingers.
Your heart will yearn
For the lovely splendor
Of the pine tree;
While rekindled fires
In my eyes
Shall wound you like swift arrows.

Memory will lay its hands
Upon your breast
And you will understand
My hatred.

—*Gwendolyn B. Bennett*

Carmen 8

Catullus! give thy follies o'er:
Ah! wretch! what's lost expect no more:
Thy suns shone bright, when to and fro
Thou, at her beck, didst come and go:
The nymph who once thy passion proved
As never nymph shall e'er be loved.
What frolic joys would then enchant,
When thou wouldst ask and she would grant!
Then clear and bright thy suns would shine:
And doth she now thy love decline?
Then be alike refusal thine.
Follow not her, who flies from thee;
Nor wretched in despondence be.
But scorn the weakness that can feel,
And bear thy grief with breast of steel.
Farewell, O girl! whom I adore!
Catullus now laments no more:
Firm he persists: he will not woo,

Nor for unwilling favours sue.
Yet wilt thou grieve, when ask'd by none,
Think, cruel! how thy days will run!
Who to thy side shall now repair?
In whose fond eyes shalt thou be fair?
Whom wilt thou for thy lover choose?
Whose shall they call thee? false one! whose?
Who shall thy darted kisses sip,
While thy keen love-bites scar his lip?
But thou, Catullus! scorn to feel:
Persist—and let thy heart be steel.

—*Catullus (Translated by Elton)*

"Farewell ungrateful traitor"

Farewell ungrateful traitor,
   Farewell my perjured swain,
Let never injured creature
   Believe a man again.
The pleasure of possessing
Surpasses all expressing,
But 'tis too short a blessing,
   And love too long a pain.

'Tis easy to deceive us
   In pity of your pain,
But when we love you leave us
   To rail at you in vain.
Before we have described it,
There is no bliss beside it,
But she that once has tried it
   Will never love again.

The passion you pretended
  Was only to obtain,
But when the charm is ended
  The charmer you disdain.
Your love by ours we measure
Till we have lost our treasure,
But dying is a pleasure,
  When living is a pain.

—*John Dryden*

To an Inconstant One

I loved thee once; I'll love no more-
   Thine be the grief as is the blame;
Thou art not what thou wast before,
   What reason I should be the same?
     He that can love unloved again,
     Hath better store of love than brain:
   God send me love my debts to pay,
   While unthrifts fool their love away!

Nothing could have my love o'erthrown
   If thou hadst still continued mine;
Yea, if thou hadst remain'd thy own,
   I might perchance have yet been thine.
     But thou thy freedom didst recall
     That it thou might elsewhere enthral:
   And then how could I but disdain
   A captive's captive to remain?

When new desires had conquer'd thee
   And changed the object of thy will,
It had been lethargy in me,
   Not constancy, to love thee still.
     Yea, it had been a sin to go
     And prostitute affection so:
   Since we are taught no prayers to say
   To such as must to others pray.

Yet do thou glory in thy choice—
   Thy choice of his good fortune boast;
I'll neither grieve nor yet rejoice
   To see him gain what I have lost:
     The height of my disdain shall be
     To laugh at him, to blush for thee;
   To love thee still, but go no more
   A-begging at a beggar's door.

—*Sir Robert Ayton*

Bonny Barbara Allan

It was in and about the Martinmas time,
   When the green leaves were a-falling,
That Sir John Graeme in the west country
   Fell in love with Barbara Allan.

He sent his man down through the town,
   To the place where she was dwelling,
O haste, and come to my master dear,
   Gin ye be Barbara Allan.

O hooly, hooly rose she up,
   To the place where he was lying,
And when she drew the curtain by,
   Young man, I think you're dying.

O it's I'm sick, and very very sick,
   And 'tis a' for Barbara Allan.
O the better for me ye's never be,
   Tho' your heart's blood were a-spilling.

O dinna ye mind, young man, said she,
   When ye was in the tavern a-drinking,
That ye made the healths gae round and
 round,
   And slighted Barbara Allan?

He turn'd his face unto the wall,
   And death was with him dealing;
Adieu, adieu, my dear friends all,
   And be kind to Barbara Allan.

—*Anonymous*

Song

You wrong me, Strephon, when you say
    I'me Jealous or Severe,
  Did I not see you Kiss and Play
    With all you came a-neer?
Say, did I ever Chide for this,
    Or cast one Jealous Eye
On the bold Nymphs that snatch'd my Bliss
    While I stood wishing by?

Yet though I never disapprov'd
    This modish Liberty,
I thought in them you only lov'd
    Change and Variety:
I vainly thought my Charms so strong,
    And you so much my Slave,
No Nymph had Pow'r to do me Wrong,
    Or break the Chains I gave.

But when you seriously Address
   With all your winning Charms
Unto a Servile Shepherdess,
   I'le throw you from my Arms:
I'de rather chuse you should make Love
   To every Face you see,
Than Mopsa's dull Admirer prove
   And let Her Rival me.

—*Ephelia*

My Pretty Rose Tree

A flower was offered to me,
Such a flower as May never bore;
But I said "I've a Pretty Rose-tree,"
And I passed the sweet flower o'er.

Then I went to my Pretty Rose-tree,
To tend her by day and by night;
But my Rose turned away with jealousy,
And her thorns were my only delight.

—*William Blake*

Neutral Tones

We stood by a pond that winter day,
And the sun was white, as though chidden of God,
And a few leaves lay on the starving sod;
    —They had fallen from an ash, and were gray.

Your eyes on me were as eyes that rove
Over tedious riddles of years ago;
And some words played between us to and fro
    On which lost the more by our love.

The smile on your mouth was the deadest thing
Alive enough to have strength to die;
And a grin of bitterness swept thereby
    Like an ominous bird a-wing. . . .

Since then, keen lessons that love deceives,
And wrings with wrong, have shaped to me
Your face, and the God-curst sun, and a tree,
    And a pond edged with grayish leaves.

—*Thomas Hardy*

Annabel Lee

It was many and many a year ago,
  In a kingdom by the sea,
That a maiden there lived whom you may know
  By the name of Annabel Lee;
And this maiden she lived with no other
    thought
  Than to love and be loved by me.

She was a child and *I* was a child
  In this kingdom by the sea,
But we loved with a love that was more than
  love—
  I and my Annabel Lee,
With a love that the wingèd seraphs of heaven
  Coveted her and me.

And this was the reason that, long ago,
   In this kingdom by the sea,
A wind blew out of a cloud by night
   Chilling my Annabel Lee;
So that her highborn kinsmen came
   And bore her away from me,
To shut her up in a sepulchre
   In this kingdom by the sea.

The angels, not half so happy in heaven,
   Went envying her and me:
Yes! that was the reason (as all men know,
   In this kingdom by the sea)
That the wind came out of the cloud, chilling
   And killing my Annabel Lee.

But our love it was stronger by far than the love
　　Of those who were older than we—
　　Of many far wiser than we—
And neither the angels in heaven above,
　　Nor the demons down under the sea,
Can ever dissever my soul from the soul
　　Of the beautiful Annabel Lee:

For the moon never beams without bringing me
　dreams
　　Of the beautiful Annabel Lee;
And the stars never rise but I see the bright eyes
　　Of the beautiful Annabel Lee;
And so, all the night-tide, I lie down by the side
Of my darling, my darling, my life and my bride,
　　In the sepulchre there by the sea—
　　In her tomb by the side of the sea.

—*Edgar Allan Poe*

"My True Love Hath My Heart and I Have His"

None ever was in love with me but grief.
　　She wooed me from the day that I was born;
She stole my playthings first, the jealous thief,
　　And left me there forlorn.

The birds that in my garden would have sung,
　　She scared away with her unending moan;
She slew my lovers too when I was young,
　　And left me there alone.

Grief, I have cursed thee often—now at last
　　To hate thy name I am no longer free;
Caught in thy bony arms and prisoned fast,
　　I love no love but thee.

—*Mary Coleridge*

Down by the Salley Gardens

Down by the salley gardens my love and I did
   meet;
She passed the salley gardens with little snow-
   white feet.
She bid me take love easy, as the leaves grow on
   the tree;
But I, being young and foolish, with her would
   not agree.
In a field by the river my love and I did stand,
And on my leaning shoulder she laid her snow-
   white hand.
She bid me take life easy, as the grass grows on
   the weirs;
But I was young and foolish, and now am full of
   tears.

—*W. B. Yeats*

DISAVOWAL

Farewell, Love

Farewell, love, and all thy laws for ever,
Thy baited hooks shall tangle me no more;
Senec and Plato call me from thy lore
To perfect wealth, my wit for to endeavor,
In blind error when I did persever,
Thy sharp repulse that pricketh aye so sore
Hath taught me to set in trifles no store,
And scape forth, since liberty is lever.
Therefore, farewell! Go trouble younger hearts,
And in me claim no more authority;
With idle youth go use thy property,
And thereon spend thy many brittle darts.
For hitherto though I have lost my time,
Me lusteth no longer rotten boughs to climb.

—*Sir Thomas Wyatt*

Farewell, False Love

Farewell, false love, the oracle of lies,
A mortal foe and enemy to rest;
An envious boy, from whom all cares arise,
A bastard vile, a beast with rage possessed;
A way of error, a temple full of treason,
In all effects contrary unto reason.

A poisoned serpent covered all with flowers,
Mother of sighs and murtherer of repose,
A sea of sorrows from whence are drawn such
    showers
As moisture lends to every grief that grows;
A school of guile, a net of deep deceit,
A gilded hook that holds a poisoned bait.

A fortress foiled which reason did defend,
A siren song, a fever of the mind,
A maze wherein affection finds no end,
A raging cloud that runs before the wind,
A substance like the shadow of the sun,
A goal of grief for which the wisest run.

A quenchless fire, a nurse of trembling fear,
A path that leads to peril and mishap;
A true retreat of sorrow and despair,
An idle boy that sleeps in pleasure's lap.
A deep distrust of that which certain seems,
A hope of that which reason doubtful deems.

Sith then thy trains my younger years betrayed,
And for my faith ingratitude I find,
And sith repentance hath my wrongs bewrayed
Whose course was ever contrary to kind—
False love, desire, and beauty frail, adieu!
Dead is the root whence all these fancies grew.

—*Sir Walter Raleigh*

from *The Adieu to Love*

LOVE, I renounce thy tyrant sway,
   I mock thy fascinating art,
MINE, be the calm unruffled day,
   That brings no torment to the heart;
The tranquil mind, the noiseless scene,
Where FANCY, with enchanting mien,
Shall in her right-hand lead along
The graceful *patroness of Song*;
Where HARMONY shall softly fling
Her light tones o'er the dulcet string;
And with her magic LYRE compose
Each pang that throbs, each pulse that glows;
Till her resistless strains dispense,
The balm of blest INDIFFERENCE.

—*Mary Robinson*

The Frozen Heart

I freeze, I freeze, and nothing dwels
In me but Snow, and *ysicles*.
For pitties sake give your advice,
To melt this snow, and thaw this ice;
I'le drink down Flames, but if so be
Nothing but love can supple me;
I'le rather keepe this frost, and snow,
Then to be thaw'd, or heated so.

—*Robert Herrick*

Song

Love, a child, is ever crying,
Please him, and he straight is flying,
Give him, he the more is craving,
Never satisfied with having.

His desires have no measure,
Endless folly is his treasure,
What he promiseth he breaketh,
Trust not one word that he speaketh.

He vows nothing but false matter,
And to cozen you he'll flatter,
Let him gain the hand, he'll leave you,
And still glory to deceive you.

He will triumph in your wailing,
And yet cause be of your failing:
These his virtues are, and slighter
Are his gifts, his favours lighter.

Feathers are as firm in staying,
Wolves no fiercer in their preying.
As a child then leave him crying,
Nor seek him, so giv'n to flying.

—*Mary Wroth*

"Farewell, sweet boy . . ."

Farewell, sweet boy; complain not of my truth;
Thy mother loved thee not with more devotion;
For to thy boy's play I gave all my youth;
Young master, I did hope for your promotion.

While some sought honors, princes' thoughts
   observing,
Many wooed Fame, the child of pain and anguish;
Others judged inward good a chief deserving;
I in thy wanton visions joyed to languish.

I bowed not to thy image for succession,
Nor bound thy bow to shoot reformed kindness;
Thy plays of hope and fear were my confession,
The spectacles to my life was thy blindness.
   But, Cupid, now farewell; I will go play me
   With thoughts that please me less, and less
      betray me.

—*Fulke Greville, Lord Brooke*

Spite of Thy Godhead, Powerful Love

Spite of thy godhead, powerful Love,
　　I will my torments hide;
But what avail if life must prove
　　A sacrifice to pride?

Pride, thou'rt become my goddess now,
　　To thee I'll altars rear,
To thee each morning pay my vow
　　And offer every tear.

But oh, I fear, should Philemon
　　Once take thy injured part,
I should soon cast that idol down,
　　And offer him my heart.

—*Anne Wharton*

"Into the middle Temple of my heart"

Into the middle Temple of my heart
The wanton Cupid did himself admit,
And gave for pledge your eagle-sighted wit
That he would play no rude uncivil part;
Long time he cloaked his nature with his art,
And sad and grave and sober he did sit,
But at the last he gan to revel it,
To break good rules and orders to pervert;
Then love and his young pledge were both
    convented
Before sad reason, that old Bencher grave,
Who this sad sentence unto him presented;
By diligence, that sly and secret knave,
That love and wit, for ever should depart
Out of the middle Temple of my heart.

—*Sir John Davies*

from *Sapho and Phao*

O cruel Love, on thee I lay
My curse, which shall strike blind the day:
Never may sleep with velvet hand
Charm thine eyes with sacred wand;
Thy jailers shall be hopes and fears;
Thy prison-mates, groans, sighs, and tears;
Thy play to wear out weary times,
Fantastic passions, vows, and rhymes;
Thy bread be frowns, thy drink be gall,
Such as when I on Phao call;
The bed thou liest on be despair;
Thy sleep, fond dreams; thy dreams, long care;
Hope (like thy fool) at thy bed's head
Mock thee, till madness strike thee dead;
As Phao, thou dost me, with thy proud eyes.
In thee poor Sapho lives, for thee she dies.

—*John Lyly*

The Broken Heart

He is stark mad, who ever says,
   That he hath been in love an hour,
Yet not that love so soon decays,
   But that it can ten in less space devour;
Who will believe me, if I swear
That I have had the plague a year?
   Who would not laugh at me, if I should say,
   I saw a flask of powder burn a day?

Ah, what a trifle is a heart,
   If once into Love's hand it come!
All other griefs allow a part
   To other griefs, and ask themselves but some,
They come to us, but us Love draws,
He swallows us, and never chaws:
   By him, as by chain-shot, whole ranks do die,
   He is the tyrant pike, our hearts the fry.

If 'twere not so, what did become
  Of my heart, when I first saw thee?
I brought a heart into the room,
  But from the room, I carried none with me;
If it had gone to thee, I know
Mine would have taught thy heart to show
  More pity unto me: but Love, alas,
  At one first blow did shiver it as glass.

Yet nothing can to nothing fall,
  Nor any place be empty quite,
Therefore I think my breast hath all
  Those pieces still, though they be not unite;
And now as broken glasses show
A hundred lesser faces, so
My rags of heart can like, wish, and adore,
But after one such love, can love no more.

—*John Donne*

The Careless Lover

1

Never believe me, if I love,
Or know what 'tis, or mean to prove;
And yet in faith I lie, I do,
And she's extremely handsome too;
   She's fair, she's wondrous fair,
   But I care not who know it,
   Ere I'll die for love, I'll fairly forego it.

2

This heat of hope, or cold of fear,
My foolish heart could never bear:
One sigh imprison'd ruins more
Than earthquakes have done heretofore:
   She's fair, etc.

3

When I am hungry, I do eat,
And cut no fingers 'stead of meat;
Nor with much gazing on her face
Do e'er rise hungry from the place:
   She's fair, etc.

4

A gentle round fill'd to the brink
To this and t'other friend I drink;
And when 'tis nam'd another's health,
I never make it hers by stealth:
   She's fair, etc.

5

Blackfriars to me, and old Whitehall,
Is even as much as is the fall
Of fountains on a pathless grove,
And nourishes as much my love:
   She's fair, etc.

6

I visit, talk, do business, play,
And for a need laugh out a day:
Who does not thus in Cupid's school,
He makes not love, but plays the fool:
   She's fair, etc.

—*Sir John Suckling*

Lament over Love

I hope my child'll
Never love a man.
I say I hope my child'll
Never love a man.
Love can hurt you
Mo'n anything else can.

I'm goin' down to the river
An' I ain't goin' there to swim;
Down to the river,
Ain't goin' there to swim.
My true love's left me
And I'm goin' there to think about him.

Love is like whiskey,
Love is like red, red wine.
Love is like whiskey,
Like sweet red wine.
If you want to be happy
You got to love all the time.

I'm goin' up in a tower
Tall as a tree is tall,
Up in a tower
Tall as a tree is tall.
Gonna think about my man—
And let my fool-self fall.

—*Langston Hughes*

"I said to Love"

    I said to Love,
'It is not now as in old days
When men adored thee and thy ways
    All else above;
Named thee the Boy, the Bright, the One
Who spread a heaven beneath the sun,'
    I said to Love.

    I said to him,
'We now know more of thee than then;
We were but weak in judgment when,
    With hearts abrim,
We clamoured thee that thou would'st please
Inflict on us thine agonies,'
    I said to him.

I said to Love,
'Thou art not young, thou art not fair,
No elfin darts, no cherub air,
    Nor swan, nor dove
Are thine; but features pitiless,
And iron daggers of distress,'
    I said to Love.

    'Depart then Love! . . .
—Man's race shall perish, threatenest thou,
Without thy kindling coupling-vow?
The age to come the man of now
    Know nothing of?—
We fear not such a threat from thee;
We are too old in apathy!
Mankind shall cease.—So let it be,'
    I said to Love.

—*Thomas Hardy*

Did Not

'Twas a new feeling—something more
Than we had dared to own before,
    Which then we hid not;
We saw it in each other's eye,
And wished, in every half-breathed sigh,
    To speak, but did not.

She felt my lips' impassioned touch—
'Twas the first time I dared so much,
    And yet she chid not;
But whispered o'er by burning brow,
"Oh, do you doubt I love you now?"
    Sweet soul! I did not.

Warmly I felt her bosom thrill,
I pressed it closer, closer still,
    Though gently bid not;
Till—oh! the world hath seldom heard
Of lovers, who so nearly erred,
    And yet, who did not.

—*Thomas Moore*

O Do Not Love Too Long

Sweetheart, do not love too long:
I loved long and long
And grew to be out of fashion
Like an old song.

All through the years of our youth
Neither could have known
Their own thought from the other's,
We were so much at one.

But O, in a minute she changed—
O do not love too long,
Or you will grow out of fashion
Like an old song.

—*W. B. Yeats*

"Truce, gentle Love, a parley now I crave"

Truce, gentle Love, a parley now I crave:
  Methinks 'tis long since first these wars
    begun.
Nor thou, nor I, the better yet can have;
  Bad is the match where neither party won.
I offer free conditions of fair peace:
  My heart for hostage that it shall remain.
Discharge our forces, here let malice cease,
  So for my pledge thou give me pledge again.
Or if no thing but death will serve thy turn,
  Still thirsting for subversion of my state,
Do what thou canst, raze, massacre and burn;
  Let the world see the utmost of thy hate.
    I send defiance, since if overthrown,
    Thou vanquishing, the conquest is mine own.

—*Michael Drayton*

SORROW AND LAMENTATION

Bitter-sweet

Ah my deare angrie Lord,
Since thou dost love, yet strike;
Cast down, yet help afford;
Sure I will do the like.

I will complain, yet praise;
I will bewail, approve:
And all my sowre-sweet dayes
I will lament, and love.

—*George Herbert*

A Dream Within a Dream

Take this kiss upon the brow!
And, in parting from you now,
Thus much let me avow—
You are not wrong, who deem
That my days have been a dream:
Yet if hope has flown away
In a night, or in a day,
In a vision, or in none,
Is it therefore the less *gone*?
All that we see or seem
Is but a dream within a dream.

I stand amid the roar
Of a surf-tormented shore,
And I hold within my hand
Grains of the golden sand—
How few! yet how they creep
Through my fingers to the deep,

While I weep—while I weep!
O God! can I not grasp
Them with a tighter clasp?
O God! can I not save
One from the pitiless wave?
Is *all* that we see or seem
But a dream within a dream?

—*Edgar Allan Poe*

The Sorrow of Love

The brawling of a sparrow in the eaves,
The brilliant moon and all the milky sky,
And all that famous harmony of leaves,
Had blotted out man's image and his cry.

A girl arose that had red mournful lips
And seemed the greatness of the world in tears,
Doomed like Odysseus and the labouring ships
And proud as Priam murdered with his peers;

Arose, and on the instant clamorous eaves,
A climbing moon upon an empty sky,
And all that lamentation of the leaves,
Could but compose man's image and his cry.

—*W. B. Yeats*

Six O'Clock in Princes Street

In twos and threes, they have not far to roam,
   Crowds that thread eastward, gay of eyes;
Those seek no further than their quiet home,
   Wives, walking westward, slow and wise.

Neither should I go fooling over clouds,
   Following gleams unsafe, untrue,
And tiring after beauty through star-crowds,
   Dared I go side by side with you;

Or be you in the gutter where you stand,
   Pale rain-flawed phantom of the place,
With news of all the nations in your hand,
   And all their sorrows in your face.

—*Wilfred Owen*

The Soote Season

The soote season that bud and bloom forth brings
With green hath clad the hill and eke the vale,
The nightingale with feathers new she sings,
The turtle to her make hath told her tale.
Summer is come, for every spray now springs,
The hart hath hung his old head on the pale,
The buck in brake his winter coat he flings,
The fishes float with new repaired scale,
The adder all her slough away she slings,
The swift swallow pursueth the flyes smale,
The busy bee her honey now she mings,—
Winter is worn, that was the flowers' bale:
And thus I see, among these pleasant things
Each care decays—and yet my sorrow springs.

—*Henry Howard, Earl of Surrey*

The Banks O'Doon

Ye flowery banks o' bonie Doon,
 How can ye blume sae fair;
How can ye chant, ye little birds,
 And I sae fu' o' care!

Thou'll break my heart, thou bonie bird
 That sings upon the bough;
Thou minds me o' the happy days
 When my fause luve was true.

Thou'll break my heart, thou bonie bird
 That sings beside thy mate;
For sae I sat, and sae I sang,
 And wist na o' my fate.

Aft hae I rov'd by bonie Doon,
 To see the wood-bine twine,
And ilka bird sang o' its love,
 And sae did I o' mine.

Wi' lightsome heart I pu'd a rose
  Frae aff its thorny tree,
And my fause luver staw the rose,
  But left the thorn wi' me.

Wi' lightsome heart I pu'd a rose,
  Upon a morn in June:
And sae I flourish'd on the morn,
  And sae was pu'd or noon!

—*Robert Burns*

Lesbia on Her Sparrow

Tell me not of Joy: there's none
Now my little Sparrow's gone;
   He, just as you
   Would toy and wooe,
He would chirp and flatter me,
He would hang the Wing a while,
Till at length he saw me smile,
Lord how sullen he would be?

He would catch a Crumb, and then
Sporting let it go agen,
   He from my Lip
   Would moysture sip,
He would from my Trencher feed,
Then would hop, and then would run,
And cry *Philip* when h' had done,
O whose heart can choose but bleed?

O how eager would he fight?
And ne'er hurt though he did bite:
  No Morn did pass
  But on my Glass
He would sit, and mark, and do
What I did, now ruffle all
His Feathers o'r, now let 'em fall,
And then straightway sleek 'em too.

Whence will *Cupid* get his Darts
Feather'd now to peirce our hearts?
  A wound he may,
  Not Love conveigh,
Now this faithfull Bird is gone,
O let Mournfull Turtles joyn
With Loving Red-breasts, and combine
To sing Dirges o'r his Stone.

—*William Cartwright*

To Mrs. M. A. Upon Absence

'Tis now since I began to die
Four months, yet still I gasping live;
Wrapp'd up in sorrow do I lie,
  Hoping, yet doubting a reprieve.
Adam from Paradise expell'd
Just such a wretched being held.

'Tis not thy love I fear to lose,
  That will in spite of absence hold;
But 'tis the benefit and use
  Is lost, as in imprison'd gold:
Which though the sum be ne'er so great,
Enriches nothing but conceit.

What angry star then governs me
  That I must feel a double smart,
Prisoner to fate as well as thee;
  Kept from thy face, link'd to thy heart?
Because my love all love excels,
Must my grief have no parallels?

Sapless and dead as Winter here
   I now remain, and all I see
Copies of my wild state appear,
   But I am their epitome.
Love me no more, for I am grown
Too dead and dull for thee to own.

—*Katherine Philips*

The Maid's Lament

I loved him not; and yet, now he is gone,
   I feel I am alone.
I checked him while he spoke; yet could he speak,
   Alas! I would not check.
For reasons not to love him once I sought,
   And wearied all my thought
To vex myself and him: I now would give
   My love, could he but live
Who lately lived for me, and, when he found
   'Twas vain, in holy ground

He hid his face amid the shades of death!
   I waste for him my breath
Who wasted his for me! but mine returns,
   And this lorn bosom burns
With stifling heat, heaving it up in sleep,
   And waking me to weep

Tears that had melted his soft heart: for years
    Wept he as bitter tears!
Merciful God! such was his latest prayer,
    These may she never share.
Quieter is his breath, his breast more cold,
    Than daisies in the mould,
Where children spell, athwart the churchyard
        gate,
    His name and life's brief date.
Pray for him, gentle souls, whoe'er you be,
    And, oh! pray too for me!

—*Walter Savage Landor*

Upon the Loss of His Mistresses

I have lost, and lately, these
Many dainty mistresses:
Stately *Julia*, prime of all;
Sappho next, a principal:
Smooth *Anthea*, for a skin
White and heaven-like crystalline:
Sweet *Electra*, and the choice
Myrrha, for the lute and voice:
Next *Corinna*, for her wit,
And the graceful use of it:
With *Perilla*: all are gone;
Only Herrick's left alone
For to number sorrow by
Their departures hence, and die.

—*Robert Herrick*

Marriage

No more alone sleeping, no more alone waking,
  Thy dreams divided, thy prayers in twain;
Thy merry sisters to-night forsaking,
  Never shall we see thee, maiden, again.

Never shall we see thee, thine eyes glancing,
  Flashing with laughter and wild in glee,
Under the mistletoe kissing and dancing,
  Wantonly free.

There shall come a matron walking sedately,
  Low-voiced, gentle, wise in reply.
Tell me, O tell me, can I love her greatly?
  All for her sake must the maiden die!

—*Mary Coleridge*

"Whoso list to hunt, I know where is an hind"

Whoso list to hunt, I know where is an hind,
But as for me, alas, I may no more;
The vain travail hath wearied me so sore,
I am of them that farthest come behind.
Yet may I by no means my wearied mind
Draw from the deer, but as she fleeth afore
Fainting I follow; I leave off therefore,
Since in a net I seek to hold the wind.
Who list her hunt, I put him out of doubt,
As well as I, may spend his time in vain.
And graven with diamonds in letters plain,
There is written her fair neck round about,
"Noli me tangere, for Caesar's I am,
And wild for to hold, though I seem tame."

—*Sir Thomas Wyatt*

The Mower's Song

1

   My mind was once the true survey
   Of all these meadows fresh and gay,
   And in the greenness of the grass
   Did see its hopes as in a glass;
   When Juliana came, and she
What I do to the grass, does to my thoughts
     and me.

2

   But these, while I with sorrow pine,
   Grew more luxuriant still and fine,
   That not one blade of grass you spied,
   But had a flower on either side;
   When Juliana came, and she
What I do to the grass, does to my thoughts
     and me.

3

    Unthankful meadows, could you so
    A fellowship so true forgo,
    And in your gaudy May-games meet,
    While I lay trodden under feet?
    When Juliana came, and she
What I do to the grass, does to my thoughts
    and me.

4

    But what you in compassion ought,
    Shall now by my revenge be wrought:
    And flowers, and grass, and I and all,
    Will in one common ruin fall.
    For Juliana comes, and she
What I do to the grass, does to my thoughts
    and me.

5
    And thus, ye meadows, which have been
    Companions of my thoughts more green,
    Shall now the heraldry become
    With which I shall adorn my tomb;
    For Juliana comes, and she
What I do to the grass, does to my thoughts
      and me.

—*Andrew Marvell*

from *Art*

"What precious thing are you making fast
In all these silken lines?
And where and to whom will it go at last?
Such subtle knots and twines!"

"I am tying up all my love in this,
With all its hopes and fears,
With all its anguish and all its bliss,
And its hours as heavy as years.

"I am going to send it afar, afar,
To I know not where above;
To that sphere beyond the highest star
Where dwells the soul of my Love.

"But in vain, in vain, would I make it fast
With countless subtle twines;
Forever its fire breaks out at last,
And shrivels all the lines."

—*James Thomson*

When I Was
One-And-Twenty

When I was one-and-twenty
  I heard a wise man say,
"Give crowns and pounds and guineas
  But not your heart away;
Give pearls away and rubies
  But keep your fancy free."
But I was one-and-twenty,
  No use to talk to me.

When I was one-and-twenty
  I heard him say again,
"The heart out of the bosom
  Was never given in vain;
'Tis paid with sighs a plenty
  And sold for endless rue."
And I am two-and-twenty,
  And oh, 'tis true, 'tis true.

—*A. E. Housman*

It Never Looks
Like Summer

'It never looks like summer here
   On Beeny by the sea.'
But though she saw its looks as drear,
   Summer it seemed to me.

It never looks like summer now
   Whatever weather's there;
But ah, it cannot anyhow,
   On Beeny or elsewhere!

—*Thomas Hardy*

Snowfall

"She can't be unhappy," you said,
  "The smiles are like stars in her eyes,
And her laugh is thistledown
  Around her low replies."
"Is she unhappy?" you said—
  But who has ever known
Another's heartbreak—
  All he can know is his own;
And she seems hushed to me,
  As hushed as though
Her heart were a hunter's fire
  Smothered in snow.

—*Sara Teasdale*

"Silent as spring rain"

Silent as spring rain
on a marsh,
my tears
fall to my sleeves
unheard by him.

—*Ono No Komachi*

TENDERNESS ～

The Pity of Love

A pity beyond all telling
Is hid in the heart of love:
The folk who are buying and selling,
The clouds on their journey above,
The cold wet winds ever blowing,
And the shadowy hazel grove
Where mouse-grey waters are flowing,
Threaten the head that I love.

—*W. B. Yeats*

If Ever I Have Thought
or Said

If ever I have thought or said
In all the seasons of the past
One word at which thy heart has bled
Believe me, it will be the last.

The tides of life are deep and wide,
The currents swift to bear apart
E'en kindred ships; but from thy side
I pray my sail may never start.

If, in the turning day and night
Of this our earth, our little year,
Thou shalt have lost me from thy sight
Across the checkered spaces drear,

Thy words are uttered; and the mind
Accustomed, cannot all forget;
While written in my heart I find
An impulse that is deeper yet.

We love but never know the things,
To value them, that nearest stand.
The heart that travels seaward brings
The dearest treasure home to land.

—*Philip Henry Savage*

from *The Princess*

Now sleeps the crimson petal, now the white;
Nor waves the cypress in the palace walk;
Nor winks the gold fin in the porphyry font:
The fire-fly wakens: waken thou with me.

Now droops the milkwhite peacock like a
    ghost,
And like a ghost she glimmers on to me.

Now lies the earth all Danaë to the stars,
And all thy heart lies open onto me.

Now slides the silent meteor on, and leaves
A shining furrow, as thy thoughts in me.

Now folds the lily all her sweetness up,
And slips into the bosom of the lake:
So fold thyself, my dearest, thou, and slip
Into my bosom and be lost in me.

—*Alfred, Lord Tennyson*

To Jane

The keen stars were twinkling,
And the fair moon was rising among them,
   Dear Jane.
The guitar was tinkling,
   But the notes were not sweet till you sung
   them
      Again.

As the moon's soft splendour
O'er the faint cold starlight of Heaven
   Is thrown,
   So your voice most tender
To the strings without soul had then given
   Its own.

The stars will awaken,
Though the moon sleep a full hour later
    To-night;
  No leaf will be shaken
Whilst the dews of your melody scatter
    Delight.

  Though the sound overpowers,
Sing again, with your dear voice revealing
  A tone

  Of some world far from ours,
Where music and moonlight and feeling
    Are one.

—*Percy Bysshe Shelley*

Serenade

So sweet the hour, so calm the time,
I feel it more than half a crime,
When Nature sleeps and stars are mute,
To mar the silence ev'n with lute.
At rest on ocean's brilliant dyes
An image of Elysium lies:
Seven Pleaiades entranced in Heaven,
Form in the deep another seven:
Endymion nodding from above
Sees in the sea a second love.
Within the valleys dim and brown,
And on the spectral mountain's crown,
The wearied light is dying down,
And earth, and stars, and sea, and sky
Are redolent of sleep, as I
Am redolent of thee and thine
Enthralling love, my Adeline.

—*Edgar Allan Poe*

"Bright star, would I were stedfast as thou art"

Bright star, would I were stedfast as thou art—
   Not in lone splendor hung aloft the night,
And watching, with eternal lids apart,
   Like nature's patient, sleepless eremite,
The moving waters at their priestlike task
   Of pure ablution round earth's human shores,
Or gazing on the new soft-fallen mask
   Of snow upon the mountains and the moors;
No—yet still stedfast, still unchangeable,
   Pillow'd upon my fair love's ripening breast,
To feel for ever its soft swell and fall,
   Awake for ever in a sweet unrest,
Still, still to hear her tender-taken breath,
And so live ever—or else swoon to death.

—*John Keats*

The Presence of Love

And in Life's noisiest hour,
There whispers still the ceaseless Love of Thee,
The heart's *Self-solace* and soliloquy.

  You mould my Hopes, you fashion me within;
  And to the leading Love-throb in the Heart
  Thro' all my Being, thro' my pulses beat;
  You lie in all my many Thoughts, like Light,
  Like the fair light of Dawn, or summer Eve
  On rippling Stream, or cloud-reflecting Lake.
And looking to the Heaven, that bends above you,
How oft! I bless the Lot, that made me love you.

—*Samuel Taylor Coleridge*

If Thou Must Love Me

If thou must love me, let it be for nought
Except for love's sake only. Do not say
"I love her for her smile . . . her look . . . her way
Of speaking gently, . . . for a trick of thought
That falls in well with mine, and certes brought
A sense of pleasant ease on such a day"—
For these things in themselves, Beloved, may
Be changed, or change for thee,—and love, so
    wrought,
May be unwrought so. Neither love me for
Thine own dear pity's wiping my cheeks dry,
A creature might forget to weep who bore
Thy comfort long, and lose thy love thereby.
But love me for love's sake, that evermore
Thou may'st love on, through love's eternity.

—*Elizabeth Barrett Browning*

Love Poem

My clumsiest dear, whose hands shipwreck vases,
At whose quick touch all glasses chip and ring,
Whose palms are bulls in china, burs in linen,
And have no cunning with any soft thing

Except all ill-at-ease fidgeting people:
The refugee uncertain at the door
You make at home; deftly you steady
The drunk clambering on his undulant floor.

Unpredictable dear, the taxi drivers' terror,
Shrinking from far headlights pale as a dime
Yet leaping before red apoplectic streetcars—
Misfit in any space. And never on time.

A wrench in clocks and the solar system. Only
With words and people and love you move at ease.
In traffic of wit expertly manoeuvre
And keep us, all devotion, at your knees.

Forgetting your coffee spreading on our flannel,
Your lipstick grinning on our coat,
So gayly in love's unbreakable heaven
Our souls on glory of spilt bourbon float.

Be with me, darling, early and late. Smash glasses—
I will study wry music for your sake.
For should your hands drop white and empty
All the toys of the world would break.

—*John Frederick Nims*

My Star

All that I know
Of a certain star,
Is, it can throw
(Like the angled spar)
Now a dart of red,
Now a dart of blue,
Till my friends have said
They would fain see, too,
My star that dartles the red and the blue!

Then it stops like a bird; like a flower, hangs
  furled:
    They must solace themselves with the
    Saturn above it.
What matter to me if their star is a world?
    Mine has opened its soul to me; therefore I
    love it.

—*Robert Browning*

When I Heard at the Close of Day

When I heard at the close of day how my name
    had been receiv'd with plaudits in the capitol,
    still it was not a happy night for me that
    follow'd,
And else when I carous'd, or when my plans were
    accomplish'd, still I was not happy,
But the day when I rose at dawn from the bed of
    perfect health, refresh'd, singing, inhaling the
    ripe breath of autumn,
When I saw the full moon in the west grow pale
    and disappear in the morning light,
When I wander'd alone over the beach, and
    undressing bathed, laughing with the cool
    waters, and saw the sun rise,
And when I thought how my dear friend my lover
    was on his way coming, O then I was happy,
O then each breath tasted sweeter, and all that

day my food nourish'd me more, and the
beautiful day pass'd well,
And the next came with equal joy, and with the
next at evening came my friend,
And that night while all was still I heard the
waters roll slowly continually up the shores,
I heard the hissing rustle of the liquid and sands
as directed to me whispering to congratulate
me,
For the one I love most lay sleeping by me under
the same cover in the cool night,
In the stillness in the autumn moonbeams his
face was inclined toward me,
And his arm lay lightly around my breast—and
that night I was happy.

—*Walt Whitman*

"When in disgrace with Fortune and men's eyes"

When in disgrace with Fortune and men's eyes,
I all alone beweep my outcast state,
And trouble deaf heaven with my bootless cries,
And look upon myself and curse my fate,
Wishing me like to one more rich in hope,
Featured like him, like him with friends
   possessed,
Desiring this man's art, and that man's scope,
With what I most enjoy contented least;
Yet in these thoughts myself almost despising,
Haply I think on thee, and then my state,
Like to the lark at break of day arising
From sullen earth, sings hymns at heaven's gate;
  For thy sweet love rememb'red such wealth
    brings,
  That then I scorn to change my state with
    kings.

—*William Shakespeare*

To Electra

I dare not ask a kisse;
   I dare not beg a smile;
Lest having that, or this,
   I might grow proud the while.

No, no, the utmost share
   Of my desire, shall be
Onely to kisse that Aire,
   That lately kissed thee.

—Robert Herrick

Appraisal

Never think she loves him wholly,
Never believe her love is blind,
All his faults are locked securely
In a closet of her mind;
All his indecisions folded
Like old flags that time has faded,
Limp and streaked with rain,
And his cautiousness like garments
Frayed and thin, with many a stain—
Let them be, oh let them be,
There is treasure to outweigh them,
His proud will that sharply stirred,
Climbs as surely as the tide,
Senses strained too taut to sleep,
Gentleness to beast and bird,
Humor flickering hushed and wide
As the moon on moving water,
And a tenderness too deep
To be gathered in a word.

—*Sara Teasdale*

He Prefers Her Earthly

This after-sunset is a sight for seeing,
Cliff-heads of craggy cloud surrounding it.
   —And dwell you in that glory-show?
You may; for there are strange strange things
    in being,
  Stranger than I know.

Yet if that chasm of splendour claim your
   presence
Which glows between the ash cloud and the dun,
  How changed must be your mortal mould!
Changed to a firmament-riding earthless essence
  From what you were of old:

All too unlike the fond and fragile creature
Then known to me. . . . Well, shall I say it plain?
  I would not have you thus and there,
But still would grieve on, missing you, still feature
  You as the one you were.

—*Thomas Hardy*

And Forgive us Our Trespasses

How prone we are to sin; how sweet were made
The pleasures our resistless hearts invade.
Of all my crimes, the breach of all thy laws,
Love, soft bewitching love, has been the cause.
Of all the paths that vanity has trod,
That sure will soonest be forgiven by God.
If things on earth may be to heaven resembled,
It must be love, pure, constant, undissembled.
But if to sin by chance the charmer press,
Forgive, O Lord, forgive our trespasses.

—*Aphra Behn*

TRANSIENCE ⟿

Passing Love

Because you are to me a song
I must not sing you over-long.

Because you are to me a prayer
I cannot say you everywhere.

Because you are to me a rose—
You will not stay when summer goes.

—*Langston Hughes*

"O lovely hand, that dost my heart enclose"

O lovely hand, that dost my heart enclose
And my whole life in a small place confine!
O hand, where Heaven and Nature both combine
Their art and ardours in supreme repose!
Sweet fingers, purest pearls of orient rose
To my wounds only cruel and malign!
Does Love permit this mercy that you shine
Unsheathed before me—Love that feels and
   knows?
O glove, most dear, most white, most delicate,
The perfect sheath for rose-stained ivory,
Where on this earth can mortal consummate
So sweet a privilege? Yield thine to me!
O fickle Fortune, O inconstant Fate,
So soon to rob the robber of his fee!

—*Francesco Petrarca (Translated by Joseph Auslander)*

"When men shall find thy flower, thy glory, pass"

When men shall find thy flower, thy glory, pass,
   And thou with careful brow sitting alone,
   Received hast this message from thy glass,
   That tells the truth and says that all is gone;
Fresh shalt thou see in me the wounds thou
     mad'st,
   Though spent thy flame, in me the heat
     remaining;
   I that have loved thee thus before thou fad'st,
   My faith shall wax when thou art in thy waning.
The world shall find this miracle in me,
   That fire can burn when all the matter's spent;
   Then what my faith hath been, thyself shall see,
   And that thou wast unkind, thou mayst repent.
Thou mayst repent that thou hast scorned my
   tears,
When winter snows upon thy sable hairs.

—*Samuel Daniel*

"Devouring Time, blunt thou the lion's paws"

Devouring Time, blunt thou the lion's paws,
And make the earth devour her own sweet brood;
Pluck the keen teeth from the fierce tiger's jaws,
And burn the long-lived phoenix in her blood;
Make glad and sorry seasons as thou fleets,
And do whate'er thou wilt, swift-footed Time,
To the wide world and all her fading sweets;
But I forbid thee one most heinous crime,
O, carve not with thy hours my love's fair brow,
Nor draw no lines there with thine antique pen.
Him in thy course untainted do allow,
For beauty's pattern to succeeding men.
     Yet do thy worst, old Time; despite thy wrong.
     My love shall in my verse ever live young.

—*William Shakespeare*

In the Middle of
This Century

In the middle of this century we turned to each
    other
with half face and full eyes
like an ancient Egyptian painting
and for a short time.

I stroked your hair in a direction opposite to
    your journey,
we called out to each other
as people call out the names of cities that they
    don't stop in
along the road.

Beautiful is the world that wakes up early for evil,
beautiful is the world that falls asleep to sin and
    mercy,
in the profanity of our being together, you and I.
Beautiful is the world.

The earth drinks people and their loves
like wine, in order to forget. It won't be able to.
And like the contours of the Judean mountains,
we also won't find a resting-place.

In the middle of this century we turned to each
    other.
I saw your body, casting the shadow, waiting
    for me.
The leather straps of a long journey
had long since been tightened crisscross on my
    chest.
I spoke in praise of your mortal loins,
you spoke in praise of my transient face,
I stroked your hair in the direction of your journey,
I touched the tidings of your last day,
I touched your hand that has never slept,
I touched your mouth that now, perhaps, will sing.

Desert dust covered the table
we hadn't eaten from.
But with my finger I wrote in it the letters of
your name.

—*Yehuda Amichai*
(Translated by Chana Blocha and Stephen Mitchell)

"I know that all beneath the moon decays"

I know that all beneath the moon decays,
And what by mortals in this world is brought
In time's great periods shall return to nought;
That fairest states have fatal nights and days.
I know how all the muses' heavenly lays,
With toil of sprite which are so dearly bought,
As idle sounds of few or none are sought,
And that nought lighter is than airy praise.
I know frail beauty, like the purple flower
To which one morn oft birth and death affords;
That love a jarring is of minds' accords,
Where sense and will invassal reason's power;
   Know what I list, this all can not me move,
   But that, oh me, I both must write and love!

—*William Drummond of Hawthornden*

Feste's Song
(from *Twelfth Night*)

O mistress mine, where are you roaming?
O! stay and hear; your true love's coming,
   That can sing both high and low.
Trip no further, pretty sweeting;
Journeys end in lovers meeting,
   Every wise man's son doth know.

What is love?   'Tis not hereafter:
Present mirth hath present laughter;
   What's to come is still unsure.
In delay there lies no plenty;
Then come kiss me, sweet and twenty;
   Youth's a stuff will not endure.

—*William Shakespeare*

To the Virgins, to Make Much of Time

Gather ye rosebuds while ye may,
Old Time is still a-flying:
And this same flower that smiles today
Tomorrow will be dying.

The glorious lamp of heaven, the sun,
The higher he's a-getting,
The sooner will his race be run,
And nearer he's to setting.

That age is best which is the first,
When youth and blood are warmer;
But being spent, the worse, and worst
Times still succeed the former.

Then be not coy, but use your time;
And while ye may, go marry;
For having lost but once your prime,
You may for ever tarry.

—*Robert Herrick*

In a Cuban Garden

Hibiscus flowers are cups of fire,
   (Love me, my lover, life will not stay)
The bright poinsettia shakes in the wind,
   A scarlet leaf is blowing away.

A lizard lifts his head and listens—
   Kiss me before the noon goes by,
Here in the shade of the ceiba hide me
   From the great black vulture circling the sky.

—*Sara Teasdale*

Now!

Out of your whole life give but a moment!
   All of your life that has gone before,
   All to come after it,—so you ignore,
So you make perfect the present; condense,
In a rapture of rage, for perfection's endowment,
Thought and feeling and soul and sense,
Merged in a moment which gives me at last
You around me for once, you beneath me, above
   me—
Me, sure that, despite of time future, time past,
This tick of life-time's one moment you love me!
How long such suspension may linger? Ah,
    Sweet,
   The moment eternal—just that and no
   more—
   When ecstasy's utmost we clutch at the core,
While cheeks burn, arms open, eyes shut, and
   lips meet!

—*Robert Browning*

Love and Life

All my past life is mine no more;
　The flying hours are gone,
Like transitory dreams given o'er
Whose images are kept in store
　By memory alone.

Whatever is to come is not:
　How can it then be mine?
The present moment's all my lot,
And that, as fast as it got,
　Phyllis, is wholly thine.

Then talk not of inconstancy,
　False hearts, and broken vows;
If I, by miracle, can be
This livelong minute true to thee,
　'Tis all that heaven allows.

—*John Wilmot, Earl of Rochester*

Midsummer

You loved me for a little,
  Who could not love me long;
You gave me wings of gladness
  And lent my spirit song.

You loved me for an hour
  But only with your eyes;
Your lips I could not capture
  By storm or by surprise.

Your mouth that I remember
  With rush of sudden pain
As one remembers starlight
  Or roses after rain . . .

Out of a world of laughter
  Suddenly I am sad . . .
Day and night it haunts me,
  The kiss I never had.

—*Sydney King Russell*

Oh, When I Was In Love With You

Oh, when I was in love with you,
   Then I was clean and brave,
And miles around the wonder grew
   How well did I behave.

And now the fancy passes by,
   And nothing will remain,
And miles around they'll say that I
   Am quite myself again.

—*A. E. Housman*

from Thomas Ford's
Music of Sundry Kinds

There is a lady sweet and kind,
Was never face so pleas'd my mind;
I did but see her passing by,
And yet I love her till I die.

Her gesture, motion, and her smiles,
Her wit, her voice, my heart beguiles,
Beguiles my heart, I know not why,
And yet I love her till I die.

Her free behaviour, winning looks,
Will make a lawyer burn his books;
I touch'd her not, alas! not I,
And yet I love her till I die.

Had I her fast betwixt mine arms,
Judge you that think such sports were harms,
Were't any harm? no, no, fie, fie,
For I will love her till I die.

Should I remain confined there
So long as Phoebus in his sphere,
I to request, she to deny,
Yet would I love her till I die.

Cupid is winged and doth range,
Her country so my love doth change:
But change she earth, or change she sky,
Yet will I love her till I die.

—*Thomas Ford*

To a Stranger

Passing stranger! you do not know how
    longingly I look upon you,
You must be he I was seeking, or she I was
    seeking, (it comes to me as of a dream,)
I have somewhere surely lived a life of joy with
    you,
All is recall'd as we flit by each other, fluid,
    affectionate, chaste, matured,
You grew up with me, were a boy with me or a
    girl with me,
I ate with you and slept with you, your body
    has become not yours only nor left my body
    mine only,
You give me the pleasure of your eyes, face,
    flesh, as we pass, you take of my beard,
    breast, hands, in return,
I am not to speak to you, I am to think of you
    when I sit alone or wake at night alone,

I am to wait, I do not doubt I am to meet you
   again,
I am to see to it that I do not lose you.

—*Walt Whitman*

A Moment

The clouds had made a crimson crown
Above the mountains high.
The stormy sun was going down
In a stormy sky.

Why did you let your eyes so rest on me,
And hold your breath between?
In all the ages this can never be
As if it had not been.

—*Mary Coleridge*

REMEMBRANCE

"When to the sessions of sweet silent thought"

When to the sessions of sweet silent thought
I summon up remembrance of things past,
I sigh the lack of many a thing I sought,
And with old woes new wail my dear Time's
   waste.
Then can I drown an eye, unused to flow,
For precious friends hid in death's dateless night,
And weep afresh love's long since canceled woe,
And moan th' expense of many a vanished sight;
Then can I grieve at grievances foregone,
And heavily from woe to woe tell o'er
The sad account of fore-bemoanèd moan,
Which I new pay as if not paid before.
   But if the while I think of thee, dear friend,
     All losses are restored and sorrows end.

—*William Shakespeare*

To F—

Beloved! amid the earnest woes
   That crowd around my earthly path—
(Drear path, alas! Where grows
not even one lonely rose)—
   My soul at least a solace hath
In dreams of thee, and therein knows
An Eden of bland repose.

And thus thy memory is to me
   Like some enchanted far-off isle
In some tumultuous sea—
Some ocean throbbing far and free
   With storms—but where meanwhile
Serenest skies continually
   Just o'er that one bright island smile.

—*Edgar Allan Poe*

Jewels

If I should see your eyes again,
   I know how far their look would go—
Back to a morning in the park
   With sapphire shadows on the snow.

Or back to oak trees in the spring
   When you unloosed my hair and kissed
The head that lay against your knees
   In the leaf shadow's amethyst.

And still another shining place
   We would remember—how the dun
Wild mountain held us on its crest
   One diamond morning white with sun.

But I will turn my eyes from you
   As women turn to put away
The jewels they have worn at night
   And cannot wear in sober day.

—*Sara Teasdale*

To Memory

Strange Power, I know not what thou art,
Murderer or mistress of my heart.
I know I'd rather meet the blow
Of my most unrelenting foe
Than live—as now I live—to be
Slain twenty times a day by thee.

Yet, when I would command thee hence,
Thou mockest at the vain pretence,
Murmuring in mine ear a song
Once loved, alas! forgotten long;
And on my brow I feel a kiss
That I would rather die than miss.

—*Mary Coleridge*

Echo

Come to me in the silence of the
    night;
  Come in the speaking silence of
    a dream;
Come with soft rounded cheeks and
    eyes as bright
  As sunlight on a stream;
    Come back in tears,
O memory, hope, love of finished
    years.

O dream how sweet, too sweet, too
    bitter sweet,
  Whose wakening should have
    been in Paradise,
Where souls brimfull of love abide
    and meet;

Where thirsting longing eyes
    Watch the slow door
That opening, letting in, lets out no more.

Yet come to me in dreams, that I
    may live
  My very life again though cold
    in death:
Come back to me in dreams, that I
    may give
  Pulse for pulse, breath for breath:
    Speak low, lean low,
As long ago, my love, how long ago.

—*Christina Rossetti*

Remembrance

Cold in the earth—and the deep snow piled
  above thee,
Far, far, removed, cold in the dreary grave!
Have I forgot, my only Love, to love thee,
Severed at last by Time's all-severing wave?

Now, when alone, do my thoughts no longer
  hover
Over the mountains, on that northern shore,
Resting their wings where heath and fern-
  leaves cover
Thy noble heart for ever, ever more?

Cold in the earth—fifteen wild Decembers,
From those brown hills, have melted into spring:
Faithful, indeed, is the spirit that remembers
After such years of change and suffering!

Sweet Love of youth, forgive, if I forget thee,
While the world's tide is bearing me along;
Other desires and other hopes beset me,
Hopes which obscure, but cannot do thee wrong!

No later light has lightened up my heaven,
No second morn has ever shone for me;
All my life's bliss from thy dear life was given,
All my life's bliss is in the grave with thee.

But, when the days of golden dreams had
   perished,
And even Despair was powerless to destroy;
Then did I learn how existence could be
   cherished,
Strengthened, and fed without the aid of joy.

Then did I check the tears of useless passion—
Weaned my young soul from yearning after
    thine;
Sternly denied its burning wish to hasten
Down to that tomb already more than mine.

And, even yet, I dare not let it languish,
Dare not indulge in memory's rapturous pain;
Once drinking deep of that divinest anguish,
How could I seek the empty world again?

—*Emily Brönte*

Surprised by Joy

Surprised by joy—impatient as the Wind
I turned to share the transport—Oh! with whom
But Thee, deep buried in the silent tomb,
That spot which no vicissitude can find?
Love, faithful love, recalled thee to my mind—
But how could I forget thee? Through what
   power,
Even for the least division of an hour,
Have I been so beguiled as to be blind
To my most grievous loss!—That thought's
   return
Was the worst pang that sorrow ever bore,
Save one, one only, when I stood forlorn,
Knowing my heart's best treasure was no more;
That neither present time, nor years unborn
Could to my sight that heavenly face restore.

—*William Wordsworth*

"If you had known"

      If you had known
When listening with her to the far-down moan
Of the white-selvaged and empurpled sea,
And rain came on that did not hinder talk,
Or damp your flashing facile gaiety
In turning home, despite the slow wet walk
By crooked ways, and over stiles of stone;
      If you had known

      You would lay roses,
Fifty years thence, on her monument, that
  discloses
Its graying shape upon the luxuriant green;
Fifty years thence to an hour, by chance led there,
What might have moved you?—yea, had you
  foreseen
That on the tomb of the selfsame one, gone where
The dawn of every day is as the close is,
      You would lay roses!

—*Thomas Hardy*

An Upbraiding

Now I am dead you sing to me
   The songs we used to know,
But while I lived you had no wish
   Or care for doing so.

Now I am dead you come to me
   In the moonlight, comfortless;
Ah, what would I have given alive
   To win such tenderness!

When you are dead, and stand to me
   Not differenced, as now,
But like again, will you be cold
   As when we lived, or how?

—*Thomas Hardy*

Love Songs in Age

She kept her songs, they took so little space,
    The covers pleased her:
One bleached from lying in a sunny place,
One marked in circles by a vase of water,
One mended, when a tidy fit had seized her,
    And coloured, by her daughter—
So they had waited, till in widowhood
She found them, looking for something else,
    and stood

Relearning how each frank submissive chord
    Had ushered in
Word after sprawling hyphenated word,
And the unfailing sense of being young
Spread out like a spring-woken tree, wherein
    That hidden freshness, sung,
That certainty of time laid up in store
As when she played them first. But, even more,

The glare of that much-mentioned brilliance, love,
    Broke out, to show
Its bright incipience sailing above,
Still promising to solve, and satisfy,
And set unchangeably in order. So
    To pile them back, to cry,
Was hard, without lamely admitting how
It had not done so then, and could not now.

—*Philip Larkin*

Tears, Idle Tears

Tears, idle tears, I know not what they mean,
Tears from the depth of some divine despair
Rise in the heart, and gather to the eyes,
In looking on the happy Autumn-fields,
And thinking of the days that are no more.

Fresh as the first beam glittering on a sail,
That brings our friends up from the underworld,
Sad as the last which reddens over one
That sinks with all we love below the verge;
So sad, so fresh, the days that are no more.

Ah, sad and strange as in dark summer dawns
The earliest pipe of half-awakened birds
To dying ears, when unto dying eyes
The casement slowly grows a glimmering square;
So sad, so strange, the days that are no more.

Dear as remembered kisses after death,
And sweet as those by hopeless fancy feigned
On lips that are for others; deep as love,
Deep as first love, and wild with all regret;
O Death in Life, the days that are no more.

—*Alfred, Lord Tennyson*

The Balcony

Mother of memories, mistress of mistresses,
O thou, my pleasure, thou, all my desire,
Thou shalt recall the beauty of caresses,
The charm of evenings by the gentle fire,
Mother of memories, mistress of mistresses!

The eves illumined by the burning coal,
The balcony where veiled rose-vapour clings—
How soft your breast was then, how sweet your
    soul!
Ah, and we said imperishable things,
Those eves illumined by the burning coal.

Lovely the suns were in those twilights warm,
And space profound, and strong life's pulsing
    flood;
In bending o'er you, queen of every charm,
I thought I breathed the perfume of your blood.
The suns were beauteous in those twilights warm.

The film of night flowed round and over us,
And my eyes in the dark did your eyes meet;
I drank your breath, ah! sweet and poisonous,
And in my hands fraternal slept your feet—
Night, like a film, flowed round and over us.

I can recall those happy days forgot,
And see, with head bowed on your knees, my
    past.
Your languid beauties now would move me not
Did not your gentle heart and body cast
The old spell of those happy days forgot.

Can vows and perfume, kisses infinite,
Be reborn from the gulf we cannot sound;
As rise to heaven suns once again made bright
After being plunged in deep seas and profound?
Ah, vows and perfumes, kisses infinite!

—*Charles Baudelaire (Translated by F. P. Sturm)*

Music

Music, when soft voices die,
Vibrates in the memory—
Odours, when sweet violets sicken,
Live within the sense they quicken.
Rose leaves, when the rose is dead,
Are heaped for the belovèd's bed;
And so thy thoughts, when thou art gone,
Love itself shall slumber on.

—*Percy Bysshe Shelley*

"Not marble, nor the gilded monuments"

Not marble, nor the gilded monuments
Of princes, shall outlive this powerful rhyme;
But you shall shine more bright in these contents
Than unswept stone, besmear'd with sluttish
 time.
When wasteful war shall statues overturn,
And broils root out the work of masonry,
Nor Mars his sword nor war's quick fire shall
 burn
The living record of your memory.
'Gainst death and all-oblivious enmity
Shall you pace forth; your praise shall still find
 room
Even in the eyes of all posterity
That wear this world out to the ending doom.
  So, till the judgment that yourself arise,
  You live in this, and dwell in lovers' eyes.

—*William Shakespeare*

Delia

When winter snows upon thy golden hairs,
And frost of age hath nipped thy flowers near;
When dark shall seem thy day that never clears,
And all lies with'red that was held so dear;
Then take this picture which I here present thee,
Limned with a pencil not all unworthy.
Here see the gifts that God and nature lent thee;
Here read thy self and what I suff'red for thee.
This may remain thy lasting monument,
Which happily posterity may cherish.
These colors with thy fading are not spent;
These may remain when thou and I shall perish.
If they remain, then thou shalt live thereby:
They will remain, and so thou canst not die.

—*Samuel Daniel*

"One day I wrote her name upon the strand"

One day I wrote her name upon the strand,
  But came the waves and washèd it away:
Again I wrote it with a second hand,
  But came the tide, and made my pains his prey.
"Vain man," said she, "thou do'st in vain assay,
  A mortal thing so to immortalize,
For I myself shall like to this decay,
  And eek my name be wipèd out likewise."
"Not so," quoth I, "let baser things devise
  To die in dust, but you shall live by fame:
My verse your virtues rare shall eternize,
  And in the heavens write your glorious name,
  Where, whenas death shall all the world
    subdue,
  Our love shall live, and later life renew."

—*Edmund Spenser*

Shirt

I remember once I ran after you and tagged the
    fluttering shirt of you in the wind.
Once many days ago I drank a glassful of
    something and the picture of you shivered
    and slid on top of the stuff.
And again it was nobody else but you I heard in
    the singing voice of a careless humming woman.
One night when I sat with chums telling stories
    at a bonfire flickering red embers, in a language
    its own talking to a spread of white stars:
It was you that slunk laughing
    in the clumsy staggering shadows.
Broken answers of remembrance let me know
    you are alive with a peering phantom face
    behind a doorway somewhere in the city's
    push and fury

Or under a pack of moss and leaves waiting in
silence under a twist of oaken arms ready as
ever to run away again when I tag the
fluttering shirt of you.

—*Carl Sandburg*

PERMISSIONS
ACKNOWLEDGMENTS

420

INDEX OF AUTHORS